THE MODERN NORTH

THE MODERN NORTH

People, Politics and the Rejection of Colonialism

Kenneth Coates and Judith Powell

James Lorimer & Company, Publishers
Toronto, 1989

To Peter Baskerville, Ian MacPherson, Bill Morrison and Eric Sager: friends, colleagues, teachers, scholars.

Front cover photos: background, Lac la Martre (Douglas Holmes); top, Rankin Inlet (Douglas Holmes); bottom, Iqaluit children (Ronnie Heming/Outcrop/Yellowknife). Inside photos: Government of the Yukon (all photographs of the Yukon); B. Wilson, Government of the NWT (Maggie Akrajuk); Tessa Macintosh, Government of the NWT (Lilliam Shamee; Dogrib Council, Snare Lake; downtown Yellowknife; NWT legislative assembly; Cape Dorset); Tessa Macintosh, Native Communications Society (Colville Lake; native home, Fort Rae; Thomas Berger; dog sleds).

Canadian Cataloguing in Publication Data
Coates, Kenneth, 1956-
The modern North
Bibliography: p.
Includes index.
ISBN 1-55028-122-4 (bound) ISBN 1-55028-120-8 (pbk.)
1. Canada, Northern - Politics and government.
2. Canada - Native races. I. Powell, Judith
II. Title.
FC3963.C63 1989   971.9   C89-094511-7
F1090.5.C63 1989

James Lorimer & Company, Publishers
Egerton Ryerson Memorial Building
35 Britain Street
Toronto, Ontario M5A 1R7

6 5 4 3 2 1   89 90 91 92 93 94

Contents

Transition (Hist)

Probs

Probs

Choice

Acknowledgements

One incurs many debts in the process of research, writing and publishing a book. We take great pleasure in acknowledging the assistance and support of many people. Barbara Kelcey helped with the initial stages of the research. One good friend, Brenda Clark, took a great interest in the project and provided invaluable advice. W.R. Morrison, as always, was of great help with the project — from concept to proofreading. His friendship and scholarship are greatly appreciated. Thanks, too, to Curtis Fahey, our patient, understanding and supportive editor. Much credit for the book's logic and presentation properly belongs to Curtis.

We must also — and enthusiastically — thank our families. Dennis, Shān and Mark Powell provided unflagging support and encouragement, and were remarkably understanding of frequent absences from home. The Coates family have, again, been tremendous. Cathy's support and enthusiasm remain unbroken. Bradley, Mark and Laura still wonder why Dad spends so much time with his word processor. May they one day understand — and agree the time was well-spent.

Kenneth Coates
Judith Powell
1989

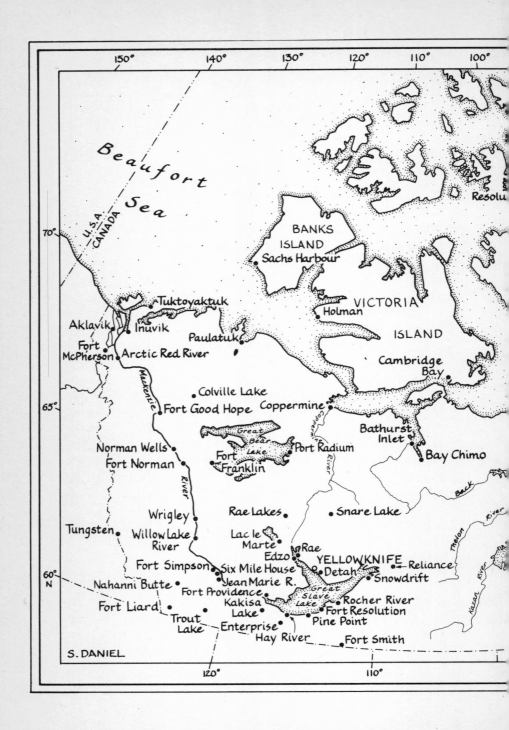

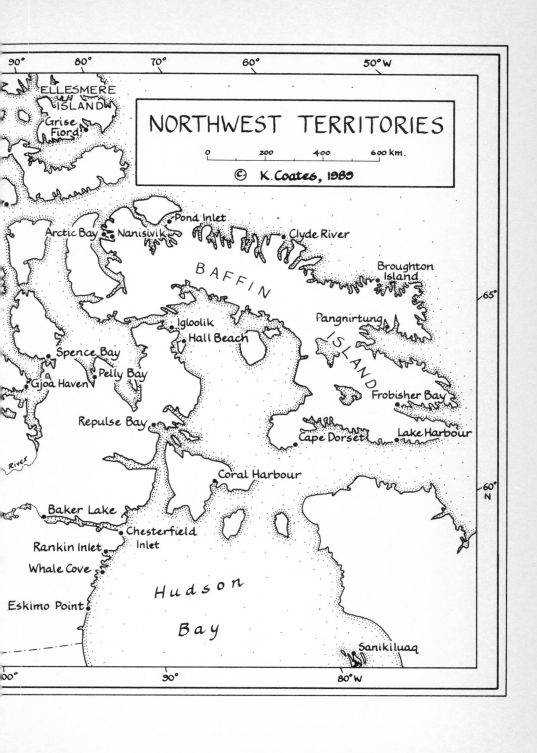

NORTHWEST TERRITORIES

0   200   400   600 km.

© K. Coates, 1989

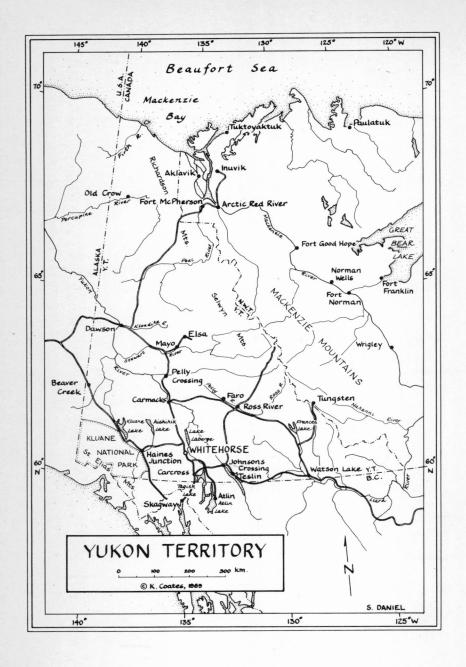

YUKON TERRITORY

0   100   200   300 km.

© K. Coates, 1989

N

S. DANIEL

Prologue

The North in Transition

The matter seemed simple enough. There was oil and natural gas on the Alaskan north slope, and similar discoveries were anticipated in the Canadian Beaufort Sea. The rich deposits were, of course, hundreds of miles from potential markets in southern Canada and the United States, but in the OPEC-fired hysteria of the early 1970s, such physical barriers seemed surmountable. Canada and the United States were scrambling to secure a supply of oil. Canadian Arctic Gas Pipeline, a consortium of multi-nationals, announced plans to build a pipeline from the Arctic slope to the transmission grid in Alberta, promising at the same time to free North America from its dependence on OPEC oil and to usher in a new era of development and growth for the Canadian northwest and Alaska.

The project found many supporters — in the Canadian oil patch, among central Canadian business people, with the mega-project oriented Liberal government in Ottawa and with Canadian and American consumers. But not everyone was pleased. The proposed pipeline would cross hundreds of miles of ecologically sensitive territory, and threatened to disrupt the aboriginal residents' already tenuous harvesting-based lifestyle. Many northern Canadians, only too familiar with the entrenched pattern of regional needs being dismissed in the name of "national interest," were concerned about the lack of consultation and northern involvement in the project. The loudest protest came from the Native organizations, many of them newly formed in response to the political and environmental pressures being imposed on them in the late 1960s. They demanded an opportunity to examine the proposal and to express their concerns about what was one of the largest commercial enterprises ever proposed.

Responding to these pressures, the Canadian government announced the establishment of the Mackenzie Valley Pipeline Inquiry in March 1974. The Trudeau administration selected Mr. Justice Thomas Berger, an outspoken defender of aboriginal rights, short-lived leader of the New Democratic Party of British Columbia and highly regarded human rights advocate, to head the commission. Neither Ottawa nor the various interest groups knew quite what Berger had in mind, for the Mackenzie Valley Pipeline Inquiry quickly distanced itself from the dyspeptic, formal and boring model of most Canadian royal commissions. If the Trudeau administration hoped for a quick and technical adjudication of the Canadian Arctic Gas application, they had picked the wrong man for the task. Berger's investigation proved to be passionate, intensive, controversial and wide-ranging.

Through the summer and fall of 1974, Berger and his commission, accompanied by a brigade of journalists, lawyers, government officials, representatives from Native organizations and "interveners" (the scientists, economists, sociologists and anthropologists who commented on the potential impact of the proposed pipeline) travelled across Canada and throughout the North. This commission spurned hotel conference rooms and the comfortable surroundings of the city for school gymnasiums in isolated sub-Arctic and Arctic communities. In village after village, Berger listened patiently and attentively, adapting the commission format admirably to suit the very different speaking style of the Dene people. While he gave full due to the pipeline promoters and their witnesses — the commission files are laden with dozens of highly technical reports covering all aspects of pipeline design, construction and maintenance — it was Berger's attention to the words and passions of the northern Indians that caught the attention of the Canadian public.

Those were most unusual times. Night after night, radio, television and newspaper reporters described the expedition and captured the special emotions of the Dene. The journalists recognized the unique circumstances they were witnessing; one of their number, the CBC's Whit Fraser, went so far as to step forward as a witness on the Indians' behalf near the end of the inquiry. The pipeline advocates were angered, both by what they perceived as the media's bias against their project and the increasingly non-technical tone of the inquiry. They had hoped and asked for an examination of the economic and technical feasibility of their project. They had anticipated challenges on environmental grounds, and had prepared a battery of reports and witnesses to counter such criticism. They had not, however, counted on the simple eloquence of Dene speakers, describing their attachment to the land and the animals, and telling of their own special relationship with the environment.

The final report, submitted to the Canadian government in April 1977, became an overnight bestseller, testimony to Canadians' fascination with the work of Thomas Berger. For followers of the inquiry, there were few surprises. Berger advocated a postponement of the pipeline project for ten years (and recommended an examination of the Alaska Highway option advanced by Foothills Pipeline), urged the government to settle northern Native land claims and called for measures to protect the sub-Arctic environment, most notably through the establishment of a national park or wildlife reserve in the northern Yukon. Berger had produced a remarkable document, *Northern Frontier, Northern Homeland* — although not all readers, to be sure, were pleased with the recommendations. The federal government, feeling the heat of public pressure, shelved the pipeline project.

Much has happened in the years since the Mackenzie Valley Pipeline Inquiry. Native land claims are on the verge of being settled. The federal government has negotiated a final settlement covering the Western Arctic with the Committee for Original Peoples Entitlement (COPE) and framework agreements with the Dene/Metis of the Mackenzie River Valley and the Council of Yukon Indians. On the pipeline front, after the demise of the

Mackenzie Valley project, attention shifted to the Alaska Highway proposal, backed by Alberta's Bob Blair, and it appeared for
a short time as though construction would actually proceed. But
declining world prices for natural gas undermined the financial
viability of the project and it remains officially on hold. The
northern Yukon national park concept, one of Berger's recommendations that found much public favour, was pushed
through. Meanwhile, in the Beaufort Sea, several promising oil
strikes were made, financed through generous federal government subsidies, and development appeared imminent. However,
the Trudeau government's poorly conceived National Energy
Program, a grandiose plan for nationalizing the oil industry and
increasing federal returns from the resource, combined with
declining world oil prices to dampen the enthusiasm. A much
smaller oil pipeline, linking Norman Wells in the Northwest
Territories to the Alberta pipeline system, proceeded in the 1980s,
but with little of the fanfare associated with the earlier proposals.
There is now talk of reviving the Alaska Highway Natural Gas
Pipeline as well as the Mackenzie Valley pipeline.

Although it is somewhat difficult to recall the excitement and
genuine passions of the politics of northern oil and gas development in the 1970s, it is clear that the Berger inquiry represented
a watershed for the Canadian North. In the 1960s, after decades
of neglect, Canadians had just begun to pay attention to their
northland. As before, however, they did so with a view to the
benefits flowing to the south — from the perspective of a colonial
power examining the resource wealth of its colonies. The
development of major new mines — Pine Point in the Northwest
Territories and Cyprus-Anvil in the Yukon — confirmed the
national belief in the magnitude of northern riches. Canadians
looked northward with an enthusiasm hardly matched since the
days of the Klondike gold rush, but they did so with careful
attention to their self-interest.

The Mackenzie Valley Pipeline Inquiry changed this perception. The clear and unequivocal statements from the northern
Indians registered in the minds of people across the country. This
was truly their homeland, and Berger had provided a forum
through which they could take this simple but fundamental mes-

sage to the citizens, politicians and businessmen of Canada. It would no longer do to treat the North as an uninhabited appendage of the nation-state; Northerners would not stand for it and, increasingly, neither would many other Canadians.

Since the mid-1970s, the North has been set on a radically different course. Not all of the changes flow from the Berger inquiry — development schemes were in place before then, northern Natives had started to organize a decade earlier and regional politicians, led by the tight-lipped but influential Erik Nielsen, had long advocated greater autonomy for the Yukon and Northwest Territories. In the decade and a half since the establishment of the Mackenzie Valley Pipeline Inquiry, however, the North has clearly been in transition. Many of the old forces are still in evidence — control by southern-based corporations, a lack of interest among national politicians and the vulnerabilities of a resource-based economy. But there are also new influences — the power and determination of Native organizations, remarkably creative artistic impulses, educational innovation, experimentation with new political models and a search for economic and cultural stability. The interplay between these forces, new and old, occasionally complementary but often conflicting, forms the subject of this book.

The people, organizations, businesses, civil servants and politicians are re-creating the Canadian North, attempting to strike a balance between legitimate national interests in the region and the economic and social needs of the citizens of the Yukon and Northwest Territories. The struggles and developments described herein are very much interconnected. The battle for economic stability, for example, is conditioned by attempts to ensure political equality. Similarly, the recent expansion of northern-based cultural expression reflects important changes in the social and demographic structure of the Yukon and Northwest Territories. The thematic approach offered here — people, economy, territorial politics, bureaucrats, Native mobilization and northern culture — affords an entrée into the complex pattern of life in the Yukon and Northwest Territories. Since confederation, the northern Territories have been Canada's colonies; now, the North is fighting back, demanding political equality and the right to develop as its residents see fit. This book is an account of the decolonization of the Canadian North, a process that is by no means complete but which will ultimately affect all Canadians.

1

The Land and its People

Most Canadians have simple — and often simplistic — notions of life in the Canadian North, reducing the vibrant and diverse human landscape to pictures of solitary Inuit trappers travelling across the snow-covered tundra. The reality is very different. The region has a complex racial fabric, bringing together Indians, Inuit, mixed bloods and non-Natives. The communities range from isolated Native villages, built around a harvesting existence and government assistance, to ultra-modern transportable mining camps, staffed by people flown in on rotation. There are also well-supplied, contemporary communities — Whitehorse and Yellowknife — with conveniences and services unrivalled in towns their size elsewhere in Canada. Underlying this diversity is the mobility of the non-Native population and the striking growth in recent years of the Native communities.

The North has always been the most sparsely populated part of Canada. Even after the mining boom of the 1960s, the increase in population was comparatively minor in absolute terms. In 1961, the Northwest Territories had only 23,000 residents; ten years later, the population had grown to 34,800 and by 1981 the number had risen to 45,700. The pattern of growth has continued, and in 1986, the NWT population reached 52,200. The population of the Yukon Territory also grew over the same period, jumping from 14,600 in 1961 to 18,400 ten years later and 23,200 in 1981. The census of 1986 recorded 23,500 residents in the Yukon territory. While the total number is quite small — only 75,700 in the territorial North in 1986 — the growth rate is quite impressive. The population grew over eighty-three percent between 1961 and 1981, over twice the national rate for the period. The pace has continued since that time, for an additional 6,800 people have been added to the overall population (a roughly ten percent increase) between 1981 and 1986.

The population increase has not, however, been spread evenly across the northland. In fact, a strikingly high percentage of the territorial population is found in just two cities. Both Whitehorse and Yellowknife have grown substantially over the past two decades. Whitehorse, capital of the Yukon, had 11,500 residents in 1971 and over 18,400 in 1986. The latter figure represents over two thirds of the Yukon total. Only three of the other sixteen Yukon communities — Faro, Watson Lake and Dawson City — currently have more than 1,000 residents.

The urban distribution in the Northwest Territories is more even, although the capital city does dominate the region. Yellowknife, home to 8,500 in 1971, currently has a population of 11,750, and makes up over twenty percent of the NWT. Unlike the Yukon, however, the NWT has a series of smaller regional centres, each serving a sizeable area. Three communities, Iqaluit (formerly Frobisher Bay), Inuvik and Hay River, each have about 3,000 people. There are, in addition, eight other communities (Pangnirtung, Baker Lake, Eskimo Point, Rankin Inlet, Cambridge Bay, Fort Smith, Pine Point, Rae-Edzo) with more than 1,000 residents. The remaining population is scattered among another sixty-four communities, many of them isolated harvesting centres.

The past twenty years have also witnessed a marked increase in the Native population in the territories. In the Yukon Territory, the official Native population has grown from 2,400 in 1961 to 4,045 in 1981 (1,500 of whom live in Whitehorse). The Indians make up approximately twenty percent of the total population, a minority position established in the last years of the 19th century. In contrast to the Yukon, Native groups predominate in the Northwest Territories; the Inuit make up almost thirty-five percent of the total population, while the Dene account for an additional twenty-three percent. There is, again in contrast to the Yukon, also a substantial Metis (or mixed-blood) population, which is culturally and politically distinct from other aboriginal groups in the territory. The Inuit form an absolute majority in the eastern Arctic, while the Dene and Metis constitute a substantial minority in the western Northwest Territories.

The North is also a young region. Few people, except for the Natives, retire in the area; conversely, the pervasiveness of the frontier myth ensures a steady northward migration of young non-Native people looking for work and adventure. The youthfulness of the Native communities originates in a very high birth rate (albeit one which has been dropping over the past decade, from 35.7 per thousand in 1971 to 27.3 per thousand in 1981 in the NWT) and declining infant mortality.

The Yukon and Northwest Territories are, therefore, significantly different from the rest of the country. Many people live in government regional centres, but large numbers are scattered across the huge northern land mass, sustaining the small, harvesting villages. Native people make up a significant portion of the total population, particularly in the Northwest Territories. Much of the North, however, remains unsettled — and parts of the region are clearly uninhabitable. The people — Native, Metis and non-Native, rural and urban, government employees, miners and trappers — have found different ways of adapting to their northern location and have, in the process, created a unique human landscape in the Canadian North.

Living Spaces: The Yukon Territory

There is, of course, no single northern lifestyle, nor a single prototype of the appropriate northern community. The settlements of the Yukon Territory, as in the NWT, reflect their history, the level of government investment, their economic function and ethnic mix. The communities range from modern, well-serviced government centres to isolated, poorly developed Native villages and also include a diverse mix of highway towns and mining camps. In the Yukon Territory, there is also a striking social and economic gap between Whitehorse, the capital since 1953, and the other communities.

Beginning in the Second World War, when the construction of the Alaska Highway resulted in the rapid expansion of Whitehorse, the community has dominated life in the territory. Home to over two-thirds of the Yukon population, Whitehorse is a modern, cosmopolitan and diverse community. There are a few remaining signs of the city's origins as a company town of the White Pass and Yukon Route, particularly as weeds and shrubs continue to encroach on the abandoned rail-line that gave the community its life during the Klondike gold rush.

Whitehorse has facilities and services that one would not expect in a community twice its size. Generous grants from the territorial and federal governments have permitted the construction of impressive facilities, most noticeably the Territorial Government Building, a large, modern hospital, an impressive Justice building, a new skating rink, the North's best cross-country skiing facility and the recently opened Yukon College campus. Comparatively secure government jobs have ensured Whitehorse a full measure of prosperity, although the community suffered through a major recession in the aftermath of the collapse of the Alaska Highway pipeline project and during the downturn in the mining economy in the early 1980s.

There is, however, life beyond Whitehorse. Dawson City, service centre for the Klondike gold fields, is a particularly interesting community. The town had all but died by the mid-1960s, struggling in vain to find a replacement for the massive gold dredges that had kept the community alive since the turn of the century. The closure of the Yukon Consolidated Gold Corporation's operations in 1966 represented a potentially fatal blow. Local boosters sought alternatives, particularly through the exploitation of the city's Klondike heritage. This effort was aided substantially by Pierre Berton's phenomenally popular books on the Klondike gold rush.

The city's appeal for help came at precisely the right moment, for the federal government agreed to develop the Dawson area as a National Historic Site, ensuring a large number of seasonal jobs and a major tourist attraction. Dawson City was aided further by the surge in gold prices in the mid-1970s. The tailings left behind by the now-abandoned gold dredges, not completely stripped of their wealth due to inefficient technology, attracted renewed interest. Dozens of miners returned to the creeks. Once on the verge of becoming a ghost town, Dawson had been resurrected.

The community has since grown significantly, from 920 in 1971 to 1,552 in 1986. The population figures are deceptive, however. Many companies, including the mining operations and several of the hotels and restaurants, operate only during the summer months, when available water supplies permit hydraulic operations and the tourists are in town. Large numbers of young people come north every year to work at the various tourist attractions, including Bear Creek, Diamond Tooth Gertie's and the Gaslight Follies. Dawson continues to follow the seasonal rhythms that have so long dominated northern society; there is a considerable difference between the boisterous, active community of the summer months and the more subdued settlement of the winter.

The seasonal rhythms of Dawson City are duplicated in the Territory's highway communities, most of which came into being following the construction of the Alaska Highway during World War II. The wartime maintenance yards have long since been shut down, but several communities — Watson Lake, Teslin, Haines Junction, Burwash Landing and Beaver Creek — owe much of their existence to the highway. In the 1950s, the federal and territorial governments built schools and other facilities near the major maintenance yards and encouraged the Native people to move from their bush camps to the new settlements (several of which were located on the site of seasonal Indian camps). The Natives eventually moved into the communities, although often with considerable reluctance.

The highway communities developed around road-related services, including gas stations, small hotels and restaurants, tiny residential Native reserves, and a few government facilities, including Royal Canadian Mounted Police stations, territorial government highway maintenance shops and schools. The towns have remained very small, although the Native portion of their population has increased over time. Like Dawson, they are tied into the seasonal patterns of tourist traffic along the Alaska Highway.

The Yukon's mining communities are not tied to seasonal cycles in the same fashion, although the insecurity of world metal prices provides a different form of instability. The mining boom in the late 1960s led to the establishment of several major mining camps. Faro, base for the Cyprus-Anvil mine, was burned to the ground in 1968 — even before the first residents had moved in — but it was quickly rebuilt and occupied. Clinton Creek, located northwest of Dawson City, had opened in 1968, following the opening of the Cassiar Asbestos Company's mine. In an era of favourable union contracts and buoyant corporate coffers, the mining companies constructed modern communities, with complete amenities, for their workers and their families.

Faro, built around a central service core which included stores, a hotel and bar and a recreation complex, was the largest. In the early 1970s, more than 1800 people lived in the community, making it the Territory's second largest. As a mining camp, it attracted a large number of young men, had a very high turnover in population and suffered through the social difficulties of drug and alcohol use endemic in isolated mining camps. There was, however, a growing core of people who were interested in putting down roots in the town, and by the late 1970s the community was taking on a more settled air, boasting a population of more than 2,000. But then came disaster — the closure of the mine in 1982. By 1985, the town had only 322 residents. A revival of sorts occurred when Curraugh Resources reopened the mine on a reduced basis in 1986, but the community remained a shadow of its former self.

If fate was unkind to Faro, Clinton Creek faced an even more severe end. While the asbestos mine operated, the community looked much like Faro, enjoying new homes, a school, recreation facilities and the other services expected of a contemporary northern settlement. But in 1978, ten years after the mine's opening, it had all disappeared. The mine was closed down and the mill and other facilities dismantled. Today, Clinton Creek consists of little more than mine wastage and abandoned home sites.

At the opposite extreme from the planned, corporate-dominated communities of Faro and Clinton Creek are the Native villages. Although there has been a noticeable shift in Native population — especially young people — towards Whitehorse, many Native people remain in small, isolated Indian settlements. Old Crow, with a population of less than 300, is the most famous of these villages, immortalized in Edith Josie's widely syndicated newspaper column "Here Are the News." The community is located more than 190 kilometers north of the Arctic circle and is not accessible by road. For many years, Old Crow had few amenities beyond a nursing station, a police detachment and a school, and only recently has an effort been made to modernize housing and community services. An impressive community centre and a small subdivision of new houses have changed the external character of the community considerably. Yet this is, like Ross River further south, still a harvesting community, based particularly on the muskrat hunt in the Old Crow Flats and the harvesting of the Porcupine River caribou herd. Old Crow is, furthermore, a community determined to maintain its attachment to the land and has resisted attempts to modernize too quickly.

These community profiles indicate something of the complexity of settlement in the Yukon Territory. There is, of course, more to the Territory. Summer cabins, a few adapted for year-round use, line the shores of Marsh and Tagish Lakes, near Whitehorse. Keno and Elsa, located near the rich silver-lead deposits mined by United Keno Hill Mines, reveal the nature of pre-1960s mining camps, and show little evidence of the hand of a town planner. There are also indications that mining companies will resist the temptation to build full communities in the future; plans for mineral development in the Macmillan Pass region call for the use of fly-in camps for the workers, limiting both the start-up costs for the mine and the nature of the company's commitment to the region. The Yukon is diverse, geographically, ethnically and economically, and the Territory's many and varied communities provide an excellent reflection of that fact.

Living Spaces: The Northwest Territories

The settlement pattern of the Northwest Territories, while differing from that of the Yukon, also reveals the cultural and economic diversity of the North. Many of the NWT communities are comparatively new, creations of the post-war era, when government intervention and the removal of the Inuit and the Indians from the land occurred. There are many more settlements in the NWT than in the Yukon, befitting the Territory's larger size, greater cultural variety and widely scattered resources.

Yellowknife dominates the Territory, although not to the same degree as Whitehorse. Founded in 1934 following the discovery of gold on the north shore of Great Slave Lake, Yellowknife escaped from its company-town origins with its transformation into the territorial capital in 1967. The combination of local mining, regional transportation and administrative functions has ensured the community a major role in all aspects of the territorial economy. Although Yellowknife is smaller than Whitehorse (11,753 people in 1986), it shares many of the same characteristics: a full range of government offices, a solid base of well-paid civil servants, excellent transportation access to the "outside" and surprisingly good cultural and recreational facilities, topped by the Prince of Wales Northern Heritage Centre. And as in Whitehorse, Native people have historically been shunted to the least attractive part of town.

The massive size and the different political realities of the Northwest Territories have dictated considerable decentralization of political and administrative affairs. As a consequence, a series of regional centres have emerged, offering health, policing, educational and other services within their particular administrative hinterlands. Most of these communities originally developed for other reasons, and have had the administrative function appended since the early 1970s. Iqaluit (formerly Frobisher Bay), built at a traditional Inuit harvesting site, developed around a United States military base constructed during the Second World War. The base, and associated services, provided opportunities for wage incomes for the Inuit, who left their hunting camps to find work. Closer to Montreal than to Yellowknife, Iqaluit is the administrative base for Baffin Island. Rankin Inlet, in contrast, originated with the establishment of the North Rankin Nickel Mine, which operated from 1955 to 1962. Rankin Inlet also became a focal point for the federal government's relocation of Inuit families from hunting camps in the interior. With the closure of the mine, government-funded activities became the basis of the community's economy. More recently, the combination of resource-based activities and the establishment of the administrative offices for the Keewatin District in Ranklin Inlet have provided a more stable foundation for the community of some 1,400 people.

The other regional centres followed different paths to their current status. Though the Inuit had frequented the site of Cambridge Bay for hundreds of years, a permanent community did not take shape until the 1950s, when the construction of a Distant Early Warning (DEW) Line station attracted Inuit interested in wage labour. Federal government services followed, and Cambridge Bay began to attract many Inuit from the surrounding area. In 1981, the community was named as the base for the Kitikmeot Administrative Region. Inuvik, regional centre for the Western Arctic, is a different community entirely. It was the first planned community in the North, developed by the federal government in the mid-1950s in response to problems with the townsite in Aklavik. The government built homes, schools, administrative offices, a police station and other buildings (elevated, to avoid problems with the permafrost), all linked together by a unique "utilidor" (above ground and covered utility corridors) system. Since the 1960s, the town's economy has followed the boom and bust cycles of oil exploration in the Beaufort Sea.

The experiences of Iqaluit, Cambridge Bay and Inuvik mirror those of most of the Arctic slope communities. Because of government indifference to the Arctic and the continuation of Native harvesting, the Inuit remained on the land until the late 1950s (and in some areas, for a decade longer), although some were attracted to settlements such as Hall Beach and Tuktoyaktuk by the prospect of wage employment at DEW Line stations.

The situation changed rapidly in the late 1950s. Environmental catastrophes, leading to widespread hunger and starvation, captured Ottawa's attention. The Inuit were relocated into newly built coastal communities, where they relied on the security of welfare payments, pensions, family allowances and other secure government transfer payments yet continued to harvest the land's resources. Some of the relocations were substantial; families were moved from Port Harrison and Pond Inlet to Grise Fiord, on Ellesmere Island, an area not previously inhabited by the Inuit. This was but one of the forced migrations of Inuit from traditional settlements to new, government created communities. From the 1950s to the late 1960s, the migration from the land continued, until virtually all the Inuit had moved, at least for most of the year, into the new communities. These villages look much alike, a small number of government-built homes clustered together on a treeless shore, with a few larger government buildings, communications devices and cluttered beaches. The pain and trauma of these dislocations took their toll on harvesters separated from familiar territories. The process is now reversing itself; a number of the inhabitants of Grise Fiord, for example, have decided to return to their traditional homes, threatening the future of the Ellesmere Island community.

Not all Arctic communities are of such recent origin, although many of the others have their roots in non-Native activities. Pangnirtung, on the east coast of Baffin Island, began as a Hudson's Bay Company trading post in the 1920s. Other whites, including the police and missionaries, gathered at the site; the government opened a medical station on the site in 1927. The availability of services and opportunities for trade drew the Inuit into the community, although the major growth came after the 1950s. To the west, Inuit were attracted to Banks Island by the high prices paid for silver fox in the 1920s. The community of Sachs Harbour started in that decade, and gradually became the focal point for settlement on the island. The contemporary community of Holman, on Victoria Island, similarly had its roots in the fur trade of the 1920s, as did Gjoa Haven on King William Island, Arctic Bay and Repulse Bay. The Inuit did not, however, move into these settlements on a full-time basis until the 1950s and 1960s.

The communities in the southern Mackenzie River region, not surprisingly, have a very different history from the settlements on the Arctic slope. Fort Smith, another of the NWT regional centres, began as a fur trade post in the 1870s. Because of its relative proximity to southern centres — the community is on the 60th parallel — Fort Smith became the early administrative centre for the Northwest Territories. The settlement lost its primary role in territorial government in 1967, when Yellowknife was named the capital, but still has a population of 2,460 people, making it one of the largest settlements in the NWT.

Fort Smith's history parallels that of many of the Mackenzie River communities. Villages such as Fort Providence, Fort Resolution, Fort Simpson, Fort Liard, Fort Norman, Fort Good Hope and Fort McPherson began as fur trading posts, founded either by the North West Company or, after 1821, by the Hudson's Bay Company. The Dene surrounding these communities, which were also the site of mission churches, continued to hunt, trap and fish through much of the twentieth century, aided at times by the HBC or government relief. In the 1950s and 1960s, the combined pressures of a declining returns from harvesting and the first stages of the modern welfare state brought the Dene out of the bush camps and into more permanent residence in the villages. These communities remain primarily aboriginal — Fort McPherson and Fort Good Hope are ninety percent Dene and Metis, Fort Franklin, ninety-five percent; the non-Natives tend to be police officers, missionaries or government officials, particularly teachers.

The Northwest Territories also has a number of company towns, built around rich mineral deposits. Rankin Inlet started in this way, but quickly became a government centre with the exhaustion of the resource. Pine Point was a planned community, designed to provide amenities and services to compensate for the town's isolation. The apparent stability of this mining town ended with the closure of Pine Point in 1987.

The Nanisivik lead-zinc mine, on Baffin Island, provides the economic base for a community very different than Pine Point.

Established in 1974 by Mineral Resources International, the community consists of Inuit employees (and their families) and southern workers, who fly in on rotation. The mine itself is something of an engineering marvel, for numerous technological adaptations were required to enable mineral production at this northern latitude. As mineral production winds down, Nanisivik has been suggested as a base for an Arctic military training site.

Finally, there is the Polaris mine, located on Little Cornwallis Island. The mill was shipped into the North by boat and can be removed when the deposit is exhausted or becomes unprofitable. The mining camp is self-contained and temporary; miners are flown in and out on a regular basis.

These, then, are the communities of the Canadian North. They cover a wide socio-economic and ethnic spectrum, revealing the very different human adaptations to life in the Canadian North and illustrating the lingering impact of the major historical patterns — fur trade, mineral development and government intervention — on the region's settlement. The hamlets, villages, towns and cities, however, provide only the framework within which northern Canadians live. Within these physical spaces, the Dene, Inuit, Metis and non-Native residents have addressed the realities of life in the North and have developed distinctive strategies to suit their human and natural surroundings.

Native People

The continuity in northern settlements is provided by the Native people. While non-Natives come and go with regularity, the Native people tend to stay put, although they are not as tied to their home communities as they were in years past. Increasing numbers have left for university, gone to the territorial capitals to take up political or administrative positions or moved permanently to the south. Many of those who stay in the North continue to hunt and trap, but not in the same fashion as their ancestors. Over the past forty years, their society has been threatened by a series of difficult and painful transitions. The government-induced move into the settlements, undertaken during the 1950s and 1960s, altered the Natives' nomadic habits and transformed their relationship with the land. The villages, with their uniform houses, mediocre services and limited job prospects, offered a stark and unfriendly contrast to the traditional bush camp, but economic and family considerations made it difficult for the Natives to resist the government pressure.

The Whitehorse Indian reserve, now called Kwanlin Dun, illustrates the difficulties, and contemporary promise, of the Natives' migration into the communities. Established in the early 1900s, the reserve was moved several times to accommodate the expansion of white settlement. In the post-war era, the reserve expanded north of the city, separated from the rest of Whitehorse by an industrial area. Poorly constructed houses, built with inadequate water, sewage and heating systems (most heating was provided by wood-stoves) and limited community services contributed to an unattractive and unhealthy environment. Because the settlement was set off from the rest of the community, however, few non-Natives supported the Indians' requests for improvements.

As the Yukon Indians organized politically through the 1970s, noticeable improvements emerged. A small community hall, on-site social services, and eventually a reserve-based police force added appreciably to the quality of life. The Indians, however, were anxious to move the reserve away from what was clearly the least desirable piece of residential real estate in the city. After many months of difficult negotiations, and not without a little anger among the non-Native population, the Indians were relocated to new houses constructed by the band in a subdivision overlooking the city, a residential project initially undertaken to provide room for expansion during the construction of the Alaska Highway pipeline. The new reserve, still under construction, provides graphic evidence of how far the Indians have moved, socially and politically, over the past fifteen years.

A similar modernization is underway in most Native villages, as community centres, administrative/band offices and recreational facilities are constructed, housing is improved or replaced, and services are brought closer to general Canadian standards. In many centres, however, the ubiquitous northern log cabin remains an important part of the residential landscape, indicating that the improvement of Native living conditions still has a considerable way to go.

But the evolution of the contemporary North, with its promising political signs for the Native people, masks some stark and very real social problems. The transition from harvesting camp and nomadism to a more sedentary lifestyle was not made without significant social repercussions. The sum of those effects is just now becoming evident; the means of dealing with them remain sadly elusive.

Most Native people have not made a full adaptation to the wage economy. The major projects employ few Indians or Inuit, and then usually only when dictated by government regulation. There have been exceptions. A relatively small number of Yukon Indians found work along the Alaska Highway during and after World War II, Inuit across the Arctic accepted construction or maintenance jobs in the DEW Line stations, and the Natives near Ranklin Inlet relocated to be near the mines. In contrast, few Indians ever worked at the Cyprus-Anvil mine, despite the company's promise to seek out Native employees. Cominco's Pine Point operation similarly made few such overtures.

Since the 1960s, the federal government has made numerous attempts to address this problem. Several, like the encouragement of Inuit artists and the establishment of Arctic cooperatives (artistic, commercial, housing and others), have enjoyed considerable success. However, the federal government has been more preoccupied with imposing an entrepreneurial model on the northern Natives and has offered generous subsidies for individual enterprises — through such programs as the Indian Economic Development Fund, Special ARDA grants and the more recent Economic Development Agreements with the territorial governments. These administratively top-heavy programs — the forms and procedures are needlessly complex — include a few success stories, like the Champagne-Aishihik band's construction company, and a much longer list of failures. The difficulty, one for which no answer is readily apparent, is that there are very few realistic commercial prospects in most northern communities, and those that exist have, in the main, already been filled.

Despite these initiatives, unemployment remains endemic among Natives in the Canadian North. Native people often lack the technical skills necessary for industrial labour and still face discriminatory hiring practices in their attempts to find work. The wage gap between Natives and non-Natives indicates something of the problem. To use the Yukon as an example, in 1980 the average family income for Native people was slightly more than $21,000 (single-parent Native families earned an average of less than $11,000 per year). Yukon families taken as a whole received almost $31,000 per household. There is another trend worth noting: a sizeable number, over one quarter, of Native families earn more than $30,000 (compared to non-Native families). This group of professionals, managers and business people is increasingly separated from the much larger group — over forty-five percent — receiving under $15,000 per year. Native people do not, in general, earn as much as non-Native Northerners, although those with university degrees and advanced training find opportunities on par with non-Natives in the North.

Wage figures, however, do not include the Indians' country harvests of food and other supplies (especially hides). According to recent studies of Ross River and Teslin in the Yukon Territory, the Indians provide a substantial portion of their yearly food requirements through hunting and fishing, thus reducing their need for a high income.

The development of northern political organizations, affirmative action programs in the civil service and the steadily growing number of Indians and Inuit with advanced education have resulted in a sharp distinction within the Native communities. Those with training and the ability to move freely within the regional economy have little difficulty finding work and securing an above-average income. Most other Natives, lacking the skills and options, earn considerably less than the regional average and make up the majority of the unemployed.

The high unemployment rates are a cause of considerable despair among the northern Native population, for these both reflect and cause an ever-widening circle of social problems that affect the northern communities. Alcohol abuse is endemic across the North and continues despite strong community efforts to control consumption and availability. The widespread abuse of alcohol, not surprisingly, contributes to a distressing rate of fetal alcohol syndrome among infant children (eighty-four children were born in the Yukon in 1984 with this illness), spouse abuse, and alcohol-related criminal offences (the majority of charges against Native people involve alcohol). The problems filter throughout the communities; teenage suicide is of crisis proportions, as it is on many Native reserves across the country. The Natives are resisting this despoilation of their human capital, and have established self-help associations and community intervention programs, increasingly staffed by Native people, in response.

For the Indians and Inuit of the Canadian North, the difficulty lies in coming to grips with a changing world. Between the 1940s and the 1980s, the landscape has been transformed, communications and travel have improved tremendously and the influence of government officials has grown by leaps and bounds. The introduction of television has carried non-Native role models into the North and permanently altered the world view of all Native peoples. While struggling to gain recognition of their rights, the Indians and Inuit face the social and cultural problems of sustaining a way of life that is under attack, from within as well as from without. Those who have grown up as an administered people, born and raised in the years since World War II, have been removed far from the world of their parents and ancestors.

Non-Natives

The non-Native population of the Territories face very different challenges. Since the early days of the fur trade, non-Natives have, as a group, demonstrated little commitment to the North. Attracted by the prospects of resource riches or, more recently, high-paying jobs, they seized the opportunity to move north. Most often, the move has been temporary. This pattern, entrenched in the years following the Klondike gold rush, has plagued northern society since that time, interfering with efforts to stabilize and create social cohesion in the region.

There is no disputing the magnitude of the problem. As one analyst observed, the transiency of non-Natives in the Arctic is endemic: "About eighty percent of non-transient non-natives are prepared for no more than a few years stay in the Arctic. Some leave after building up a nest egg of cash; others, especially government employees, are transferred or promoted out of communities." Workers in the Beaufort Sea and at the Nanisivik and Polaris mines represent northern mobility at its most extreme. From the beginning of these projects, the people have been flown in and out on rotation, spending from three to six weeks in the North, usually within the confines of a company camp, and then given a furlough of equal length in the south. While technically they are northern workers, these highly paid individuals have had only a marginal impact on northern society and have returned very little to the region.

The scale of this migration is easily documented. In 1941, Native people born in the Yukon and Northwest Territories made up over half of the total population; non-Natives born in the Territories constituted only seven percent of the total. In 1971, the situation was reversed. Over forty-five percent of the total territorial population consisted of non-Natives born outside the Yukon or NWT; fifteen percent of the people were non-Natives born in the region. The Native population, in contrast, had fallen to slightly more than one-third of the total. One study of the western Arctic concluded, "The natives risk becoming a minority in what is essentially a rotating non-Native population." An observer of the mining work force in the Yukon Territory commented in 1976, "The men who come to work in the Yukon's mines are from southern Canada, the USA and overseas...the typical plan is to remain a year or eighteen months, work hard, save five to ten thousand dollars."

The reasons for the northward migrations are fairly obvious: career advancement, the opportunity to find work and the promise of high salaries. The average salaries in the Yukon, supplemented in many cases by northern allowances, isolation pay and other incentives, averaged over forty percent above the national earnings through the 1970s to 1981. Wages were less attractive in the Northwest Territories, remaining only twenty-three percent above the national average until the early 1980s, when they began to come closer to the Yukon salaries. The gap has narrowed significantly in the past five years; in 1983, the average Yukon wage was only fifteen percent above the national mean and has remained at the level through to 1986. The NWT has, in contrast, retained its comparative advantage. In December 1986, the average weekly earnings of a NWT employee were $650; the national average was $439 and the Yukon $510. There are, of course, other financial compensations, including Northern Allowances and other special benefits for northern residents.

But high wages have not been enough to keep workers in place. There are many reasons for the rapid departure of migrant labour: the cold climate, isolation, distance from southern amenities and the limits on professional advancement. The fact that mining, the cornerstone of the northern economy, is noted for the transiency of its workforce is another factor. A 1972 study, for example, identified a forty percent turnover of the mining labour force in the Yukon and NWT. That figure ranked behind those for Manitoba, Saskatchewan and New Brunswick, and was close to the Ontario average. Given the nature of the northern economy and the difficulties that Northerners have encountered in acquiring technical skills locally, a certain amount of transiency appears to be built in.

Further, the continuity in northern employment is less than optimal. Many companies shut down operations for the winter; there are few jobs available to absorb the seasonally surplus workers, forcing them to look outside for jobs. On a larger scale, the opening and closing of the major mines can bring abrupt shifts in in-migration or out-migration. As the *Canadian Annual Review* noted in 1979, "The economy continued in the doldrums. The number of people moving out of the territories during the year exceeded the number moving in by over thirteen hundred, and out-migration is always an indication of a stagnant economy."

Instability is the inevitable result of this constant turnover. In 1982, the NWT lost almost 3,300 people through out-migration, but attracted 3,900 new residents. Four years later, the trend had reversed, with over 5,100 people leaving and less than 3,300 arriving, for a net loss greater than 1,800. The pattern is similar in the Yukon Territory. In 1978, over 2,800 people left the Yukon; 2,653 entered the territory. The migratory loss peaked in 1982, when 1,200 more people left the Yukon than arrived. The trend has been reversed once again of late; in 1986, the Territory recorded a net population gain through migration of over 600 people.

Transiency among the non-Native population is nothing new; it does, however, reflect the continuing southward orientation of many Northerners. Raised and educated in the south, and with their families typically living hundreds of miles away, it is inevitable that most non-Native Northerners continue to view their world from a southern perspective. The ramifications of this, however, run deeply through the northern society. Many employers, for example, provide employees and their families with an annual trip to southern Canada, a necessary inducement to potential employees but a benefit unavailable in most other parts of Canada.

Civil servants and company officials are not alone in seeking to escape — if only temporarily — from the North. This is, in large measure, a function of the northern climate, particularly the long and often bitterly cold winter, and of the limited commercial and recreational options available in the North. Regional airlines, including the pre-merger Canadian Pacific and Pacific Western (in one of its advertisements it called itself the "northern dream airline"), enthusiastically promote travel packages to more gentler climates. In the Northwest Territories, and particularly in Yellowknife, the West Edmonton Mall, Canada's temple to consumerism, is an especially popular attraction. Regional businesses have long been distressed by this practice, and are fighting back. A September 1980 advertisement in the *News of the North* included a patriotic appeal:

> Why waste holiday time on needless shopping? Usually you can find what you want right here in Yellowknife for the same price or so little more it doesn't pay to carry it up. And when you support local business you are helping to pay your neighbour's salary.

Think about it. When last did you see a Southern retailer supporting local sports or cultural activities like most local retailers do? We've got to work together to build a strong community.

And then there is Hawaii for those in the west, and the Caribbean for residents of the Eastern Arctic. The tropical islands — in the winter months, the antithesis of the Canadian North — have long held a grip on the northern imagination. Each December and January a full-scale, if short-lived, migration takes place. Almost every winter issue of the *News/North, Whitehorse Star, Yukon News* or Iqaliut's bilingual *Nunatsiaq News* contains several advertisements for condominium rentals on southern islands, holiday excursions and packaged trips. To many, the obligatory annual holiday in warmer climates is an essential preventative measure in forestalling "cabin fever" and providing a break from a long, intense, dark and colourless winter. In this, of course, northern Canadians are little different from many other Canadians — particularly on the prairies — who similarly view winter as an endurance test. Northerners, however, pay considerably more for the luxury of southern travel.

If the cost of leaving is high, so is the cost of staying. While much is often made of the generous salaries and benefits offered to northern residents, particularly non-Natives, little attention is paid to the substantial differential between the costs of living in the North and in southern cities. Between 1977 and 1986, it cost between fifteen and twenty percent more to live in Whitehorse than Edmonton, and between ten and twenty percent more than Vancouver. Consumers in Yellowknife in 1983 paid from fifteen to thirty percent more for supplies than their counterparts in Edmonton. In both cases, the differential for food, particularly fresh produce, was and is much higher.

While there is a substantial gap between southern centres and the territorial capitals, there is also a wide difference within the two Territories. The highest prices in the Yukon are found in Old Crow, which is accessible only by air, and in small highway communities like Carmacks, Ross River and Burwash Landing. The variation is even greater in the Northwest Territories. Consumer prices in Spence Bay, for instance, are from 120 to 130 percent higher than in Edmonton; the residents of Pelly Bay, which cannot be reached by barge, pay from 130 to 140 percent more than consumers in Edmonton. The range is not always so extreme. Pine Point is only fifteen to thirty percent higher than Edmonton; isolated Grise Fiord from ninety to 100 percent higher than Montreal. Inuvik prices are from forty to fifty percent higher than Edmonton. Most communities in the Northwest Territories receive the bulk of their supplies by barge, with perishables imported by air. The much greater road network in the Yukon permits the routine supplying of the communities by truck, keeping prices down and greatly improving the prospects for resupply.

Native and Non-Natives in the Modern North

This description of the northern life has deliberately emphasized the differences between Natives and non-Natives. Historically, the two groups have lived and worked separately; only a few non-Natives, including missionaries, police officers, fur traders and government officials worked regularly with Native people. This was particularly true for Whitehorse, Dawson City, the Keno-Elsa area and in Yellowknife, where substantial non-Native settlements evolved. It was also true later, in the modern mining camps at Pine Point, Faro and Clinton Creek, where few Native people found work.

The historical relationship between Natives and non-Natives offered little cause for optimism in the 1960s and early 1970s. Many non-Natives, having had little direct contact with Indian peoples, held onto old and dated stereotypes of the Natives and found enough evidence in the North to confirm their impressions. The politicization and radicalization of the Native people did little to ease the tensions between Natives and non-Natives, and in fact added new concerns. The situation was more favourable in the Northwest Territories than in the Yukon. In the Territories, the existence of a Native majority made it important for non-Natives to seek a reasonable accommodation. In the Yukon, where the non-Natives dominated the Territory — particularly Whitehorse — the need for an accommodation did not seem as pressing.

Given this heritage of distrust and animosity, it is not surprising that tensions and fears persist. Perhaps the greatest change of the past twenty years has been the closing of the cultural and ethnic gap. The sincerity and legitimacy of northern Native land claims has found a reasonably sympathetic audience in the non-Native community — although many exceptions remain. As the Natives move closer to the general Canadian norms of dress, language, expectations and cultural baggage, the social gap between Natives and non-Natives also closes.

It is far too early to suggest that the transition is complete, that the Yukon and Northwest Territories are developing as bicultural social environments where racial and cultural differences are readily accepted. The political and legal battles of the last twenty years have, however, created a very different North. The vestiges of the old order remain, in economic sectors still closed to Native people, in communities where Natives and whites have not been fully integrated and in the still evident stereotypes held of Native people. Yet the transient non-Natives of the new North, emerging out of a different education system and a different social climate than those who came north in the 1940s, 1950s and 1960s, tend to be more sympathetic to aboriginal aspirations than were their predecessors. In this increasing openness to Native ambitions and expectations lies the foundation for a more lasting accommodation between Natives and non-Natives in the Canadian North.

The people of the Yukon and Northwest Territories are a culturally and socially diverse lot. While the changes and turmoil of the postwar world have brought many problems, faced primarily by the Native people, they have also resulted in rapid advances in the northern standard of living, although most of those gains have fallen to the non-Natives. A social and demographic transformation has clearly taken place over the last twenty years in the Canadian North.

2

The Search for Economic Stability

In 1974, as the Mackenzie Valley Pipeline Inquiry began, the economic debate seemed very basic. The Arctic Gas consortium wanted to build a natural gas pipeline down the Mackenzie Valley, offering in the process to create hundreds of jobs in manufacturing, production and construction. Initially, public concerns about the pipeline appeared restricted to matters of the environment and the technology of northern construction. Very quickly, however, the debate shifted and more fundamental questions emerged: who owned the northern resources and how should they be used?

The issue was not a constitutional one, for the federal government retained control of Yukon and Northwest Territories' resources. Rather, the argument was over the use of non-renewable resources and the age-old problem of the instability of the northern economy. Pipeline proponents pointed to the prospects for job creation and further oil and gas exploration in the North; critics, all too familiar with the region's boom and bust economy, wondered whether the North, and particularly Native people, would get enough out of the proposed developments. The debate sparked by the pipeline inquiry was overdue, for northern developers had traditionally opted for short-term returns, paying little attention to the long-term needs of the region and its people.

In the early 1970s, the prospects for a bust seemed remote. In the preceding decade, the northern economy had been developing quickly, based on a resurgent mining sector, expanding government spending and a growing tourism industry. But in the midst of the boom, there had been warning signs, most of which passed unheeded. The passage of time would prove that the unevenly distributed prosperity of the 1960s and early 1970s was tenuous at best, and hardly a firm foundation for a region that struggled for economic stability.

Efforts to create some measure of continuity in the North have traditionally run afoul of the vulnerability and unpredictability of frontier resource developments. The standard northern problems of isolation, climate, a small and transient work force and few roads and railways have been further complicated by the vagaries of world markets for northern resources, the uncertainty of government support and, more recently, the complications surrounding land claims. When times were good — and there have been some very good times over the past three decades — confidence in the North escalated and prosperity seemed assured. But when the busts hit, the dislocations were immediate and severe.

Mining

The federal government has not been oblivious to the structural problems of the northern economy. Since World War II, considerable effort and a great deal of money have been expended in attempts to smooth out the roller-coaster contours of the region's boom and bust cycles. Most of this effort, until the recent past, focused on the mining industry, a high profile sector backed by a powerful political lobby. At a time when the pegged price for gold would not cover production costs, the passage of the Emergency Gold Mining Assistance Act in 1948 provided generous subsidies to keep gold mines in production. Support for northern resource development expanded rapidly under the Diefenbaker administration. The Conservatives' loudly touted Roads to

Resources program and a wide-ranging series of subsidies to mining companies provided ample evidence of the government's commitment to developing the Canadian North.

Throughout the 1960s, the mining sector's repeated appeals for assistance found sympathetic ears. A creative and complex series of reduced royalties, incentive programs, tax concessions, tax holidays for new mines, special depletion allowances and assistance from government departments (particularly the Geological Survey of Canada) provided generous incentives for those who were prepared to speculate on frontier exploration. The Northern Mineral Exploration Assistance Program, for example, provided grants of up to forty percent of approved expenditures on northern properties. With mining companies facing comparatively few restrictions on their activities in the years before environmental awareness forced a toughening of land use regulations, development was virtually unhindered.

The framework of direct and indirect subsidies seemed to have worked, if the measure was the number of mines brought into production or the value of minerals delivered to market. Exploration companies spent millions of the dollars in the North each year through the 1960s and 1970s. Results were predictably mixed. Numerous mineral deposits were identified, but few were rich enough to justify immediate exploitation. However, this mattered little since the few that were developed — including the Pine Point mine on the south shore of Great Slave Lake and Cyprus-Anvil northeast of Whitehorse — were more than rich enough to encourage others to continue in the search.

The development of Pine Point illustrates the close relationship between private capital and government investment in the Canadian North during the 1950s and 1960s. Consolidated Mining and Smelting Company (Cominco) had long known of the existence of a lead-zinc deposit on its Pine Point property. But the distance from markets, high costs of transportation and other logistical considerations initially discouraged the company from developing the ore body. In the late 1950s, the company approached the federal government for assistance. The Diefenbaker government, trapped in the web of its own contradictory northern policies, was presented with an excellent opportunity to honour its commitments to resource development. Given the richness of the mine, company officials clearly got the best of federal negotiators.

Cominco proceeded with the project only after the government promised to build a rail link — the Great Slave Railway — to the south and to provide a variety of other subsidies. The federal administration received few concessions in return for its multi-million dollar commitment. The mine flourished from the beginning, providing Cominco with millions of dollars in annual profits within just a few years of opening.

Although a major mineral producer, the Pine Point mine had a curiously limited impact on the Northwest Territories' economy. Like other mines of its vintage, Pine Point was served by a brand-new community, built to house the incoming miners. The almost-exclusively non-Native workforce proved to be extremely transient. Operating as an isolated island within the NWT, the community maintained few connections with the rest of the Territory.

The mining community's relationship with Fort Resolution, a nearby Dene village, is particularly revealing. Although Fort Resolution was only forty-two miles away from Pine Point, the company did not significantly improve the rough trail between the centres. Neither did Cominco support a commuter shuttle service between the Dene village and the worksite, an arrangement that would have encouraged the Natives to seek work with the mine. Those wishing to work — and there were relatively few over the years — had to move into Pine Point where they found themselves isolated by the foreign lifestyle in the community atmosphere. Not until the 1970s, and under considerable pressure from Native groups and government officials, did Cominco make a concerted, but belated, effort to attract Native people into its workforce.

The pattern was much the same with Cyprus-Anvil's lead-zinc mine at Faro in the Yukon Territory. Once more, generous government assistance permitted the rapid development of the property, discovered by Al Kuhlan in the early 1960s. As at Pine Point, the mine owners provided a full range of amenities for their imported workers — heavily subsidized housing in the new townsite of Faro, handsome salaries, trips "outside" and other benefits. Local Native people, in contrast, found few jobs and many difficulties, despite vague corporate promises to make a special effort to recruit Native workers. The first mining crews, housed temporarily in nearby Ross River, came into conflict with the Native population, souring relations for years to come.

The marriage of risk capital and government investment in the interests of northern resource development had its problems, particularly for the Native people. On the surface, however, it appeared to work. With Pine Point and Cyprus-Anvil as the cornerstones of the respective territorial economies, the mining sector led a boom through the 1960s and early 1970s. The long-promised prosperity of the Canadian North seemed at hand. And these mines were not the only ones. A number of other major mines continued to operate or were brought into production in this era — Clinton Creek and Whitehorse Copper in the Yukon, and Yellowknife, Canada Tungsten and Nanisivik in the Northwest Territories. Employing hundreds of workers, and sustained by a buoyant market, the mining sector provided a seemingly solid foundation for what was perceived to be a stable and expanding northern economy.

Such promises quickly proved illusory. The greatest, and inescapable, problem for the mining industry is that development contains the seeds of its own destruction. As soon as production begins, the clock begins to tick towards the mine's eventual demise. To complicate matters further, the vagaries of international markets can, within a few months, undercut a mine's viability, forcing a short-term closure. Given the fragile nature of the northern economy, so dependent on one or two major mines, the closure of a single operation is devastating. After riding the good years of the mining boom for more than a decade, the North eventually hit the bust with a vengeance.

For the Yukon, serious problems began with the closure of the Clinton Creek asbestos mine in 1978. When Cassiar Asbestos, the parent company, opened the mine in 1967, they had projected a twenty-year life for the property. The government invested $4 million of the $21 million required for the townsite and physical plant. Plans changed almost as soon as production began. The company decided to high-grade the ore, taking out the readily accessible reserves and exploiting the asbestos deposit as quickly as possible. When the mine closed, the community shut down and all equipment was removed. The homes were also sold and moved, most of them to Dawson City. A decade after the closing of the mine, few signs remain of the once flourishing mining town of some 500 people northwest of Dawson City.

The Clinton Creek closure paled in comparison with the Yukon's problems a few years later. Many small placer gold operations, developed during the hyper-inflated markets of the mid-1970s and often consisting of little more than a bulldozer and a modern efficient sluice-bar, began to have trouble meeting their payrolls. The news only got worse as the recession deepened; in 1981, Yukon mineral production fell off by close to one third from 1980 levels. The following year, United Keno Hill mines and Cyprus-Anvil announced substantial lay-offs. Within a few months both had closed down, although United Keno Hill resumed operations on a reduced basis when metal markets improved. Whitehorse Copper ran out of accessible ore in 1982 and closed permanently. By the end of the year, no hardrock mines remained in operation in the Yukon Territory. The value of mineral production had fallen from the 1980 high of $360 million to only $61.5 million three years later.

The effects of the collapsing mining sector were soon felt throughout the Territory. The White Pass and Yukon Route got into difficulty as a result of a combination of the federal government's rejection of their request for a subsidy, the loss of the Clinton Creek business and some questionable management decisions. It could not long survive the termination of its lucrative Cyprus-Anvil contract. Rail operations were suspended in October 1982.The ripples swept through the Yukon with surprising speed. Make-work projects under the Community Recovery and NEED programs were undertaken in an effort to keep miners in Faro until the recession lifted. Other private sector companies, caught by the loss of business, laid off employees, demanded wage cuts or closed up shop altogether. As had so often happened in the past in such times, many people reacted by leaving the Territory, a stark reminder that the pattern of transiency and instability in the North had not yet been arrested.

Yukoners hoped that the 1982 Cyprus-Anvil closure would be temporary, but their worst fears were soon realized. When the mine workers were approached to accept wage reductions to facilitate re-opening, they were in no mood to be conciliatory, feeling that the company had not dealt with them fairly in the months leading up to the closure. Efforts to revive the company continued into 1985. The federal government and the mine's owners, Dome Petroleum, negotiated a two-year, $50 million package which permitted the employment of 250 people (less than one third of the usual workforce) to strip the overburden off the ore body. This plan was designed to make the mine more profitable once mineral prices rebounded. Although wage concessions from the unions sweetened the pot, Dome demanded further wage reductions and, when faced with continued opposition, locked the workers out. The financially strapped resource company, near bankruptcy as a result of its overly optimistic investments in the oil patch, tried to sell the Cyprus-Anvil mine, but found few takers. The mine was moth-balled in 1985.

As the death-watch continued, however, a saviour appeared on the scene. A small Toronto company, Curragh Resources, announced an interest in the property. After extended negotiations with Dome Petroleum, the banks, the Yukon and the federal governments, Curragh announced that the mine would reopen, on a reduced basis, in July 1986. Yet those who thought that the old order would soon return were to be disappointed. The White Pass and Yukon Route road-rail transportation system from Faro to Skagway was not re-established. Instead, over considerable opposition, the Skagway-Carcross road was pressed into year-round service to handle the ore trucks. That was it — the days of subsidized housing, recreational facilities and generous salaries had ended. Still, with the lingering effects of the international recession still hanging over the area, Curragh could offer a less generous arrangement but still attract a full, though transient, complement of mine workers. The mine was back in operation but the boom days were clearly over.

The Northwest Territories' mining economy, geographically dispersed and more diversified, provided a more stable base through the early 1980s than that of the Yukon, but there were serious problems here as well. The Canada Tungsten mine, for example, opened and closed several times during the 1980s, a sign of fluctuating markets and a diminishing resource base. The temporary closure of the Pine Point mine in 1983, however, foreshadowed more sweeping changes. As at Faro, wage concessions by the workers and government subsidies through special work grants kept the mine in operation temporarily, but the inevitable could not be avoided. Having operated Pine Point at considerable profit for more than twenty years, Cominco announced in 1987 that the mine would be shut down. Newly discovered ore reserves, particularly the company's Red Dog mine in Alaska, ensured a steady flow of concentrate to the Cominco smelter in Trail, BC, and made it feasible to close the Pine Point mine. Although the announcement of closure was greeted with the same howls of protest that accompanied the Cyprus-Anvil decision, the company remained unmoved. Houses in the community, as at Clinton Creek, were put up for sale; most were removed to Hay River.

While the North's major and established producing mines fell on hard times through the late 1970s and early 1980s, the news was not all bad. Many prospectors and investors, facing a decline in base metal prices, quickly switched their attention to the smaller precious metal deposits. Although it is often difficult to separate promoters' rhetoric from the reality of northern mining, some promising discoveries were made. In the Yukon, major corporations like AMAX, Hudson's Bay Mining and Smelter, Placer Developments and Pan-Ocean concentrated their explorations in the mineral-rich Macmillan Pass and Howard's Pass areas northeast of Ross River. Other properties, particularly placer operations in the Dawson area and the Mount Skookum mine, provided evidence that there were still profitable deposits in the ground. The news was even better in the Northwest Territories, where placer mines and the opening of Cullaton Lake, Lupin and Polaris mines combined with expanding exploration activity to sustain interest in the region.

Through this modest resurgence, it was clear that the mining companies had learned some lessons from both the great expectations of the 1960s and 1970s and the sudden downturns of the 1980s. The exceptional costs and implied commitments of the company-town approach to mineral production had been tried and found wanting. Worker, community and government pressures to stabilize the economic base clearly interfered with the logical development of the resource. By the 1980s, there were alternate models at hand, approaches to frontier mining that might well become the norm in the coming years.

The future of northern mining, particularly in Arctic regions, might well rest with the model offered by the "transportable" Polaris lead-zinc mine on Little Cornwallis Island. The entire operation (except the resource), including processing mill, dormitories and other facilities, was delivered to the island by barge. Once docked, the plant was quickly pressed into operation. Workers fly in and out of the mine site on rotation; there is no permanent community in the area, and hence no local workforce to draw on. Working conditions are formidable — winters are long and frigid — but the mine and the physical plant is self-contained, requiring few workers to venture outdoors. When the ore body is exhausted — initial projections call for a twenty-five-year life for the mine — the structures will be removed.

While the Polaris model of a self-contained mine site, operated by workers brought in on rotation from a larger, but distant community, seems to work well in isolated areas, it is less feasible when a mineral body is located near an established community. The Nanisivik development on the northwest coast of Baffin Island, near the Inuit village of Arctic Bay, represents a contemporary attempt to overcome the traditional barrier between aboriginal peoples and resource development. The Canadian government, a minority shareholder in the company (Mineral Resources International is the majority shareholder), provided thirty percent of the development costs, a total of $24 million. In return, the mine gained tangible evidence of federal interest in northern resources, helped to establish a firm Canadian presence in disputed Arctic territories and provided work for Inuit people in nearby Arctic Bay.

The Inuit participated in the construction of the mine much as other Inuit had done with the earlier nickel mine at Rankin Inlet. Just under half of the workers were Native, short of an unrealistic goal of sixty percent Native participation. But as the mine went into production, the Inuit discovered that their lack of technical skills and low level of educational attainment precluded them from many parts of the mine operation. By 1982, only one quarter of the Nanisivik workforce were Native. As was the case with other Arctic mines, the company experienced difficulties attracting permanent workers to the site; as a result, southern workers are now brought in on rotation and live in temporary company quarters. There is also a problem with the eventual closure of the mine, for as the Arctic Bay residents are drawn into the mining economy they will inevitably find themselves facing a difficult choice between continuing to work and remaining in the home community.

The economic trials of the past decade have raised new questions about mining. While exploration and mineral developments remain, and likely will remain, the backbone of the northern economy in the coming decades, mining offers at best a shaky and uneven basis for regional growth. Infrastructure investments in the major mines have proven to be of little lasting value; the Aisihik dam, built in the 1970s to provide power for Cyprus-Anvil, has been a financial albatross around the necks of Yukoners since construction began. While the new prototypes of the northern mines, based on a transient work-force and smaller, leaner operations, may be more fiscally efficient, the spin-off benefits for the region at large are significantly lower. And serious questions remain about the continued tension between Native people and the mining sector; their relationship has been uneasy and not mutually beneficial in the past. Importantly, and as will be discussed later, there are clear signs that the many questions surrounding northern mineral development are being recognized and addressed.

The Big Gamble: Oil and Natural Gas in the 1970s

By the early 1970s, the search for minerals, though of vital importance to the northern economy, had been overshadowed by oil and gas exploration. The North's petroleum resources had been long known. The identification of the Athabasca tar sands in the nineteenth century first spurred prospectors' dreams of northern oil riches. The discovery of oil at Norman Wells in 1920 again sparked great, if temporary, enthusiasm. The Norman Wells field would languish until the 1940s, cut off by distance and technical problems from southern markets. The ill-fated Canol Project undertaken during World War II revived interest in the region, but once more the promoters' visions fell far short of reality. High costs, poor planning and low production doomed this short-lived venture. Still, there was evidence of northern petroleum; the time was simply not yet right for development.

Although exploration continued, aided once more by generous federal incentives, enthusiasm for frontier oil properties remained in check, particularly in the oil-rich 1960s. But the 1968 discovery of the massive Prudhoe Bay field, estimated at ten billion barrels of oil and twenty-five trillion cubic feet of natural gas, altered the equation considerably. After the attempt by the *Manhattan* to discover the suitability of tanker travel through the Northwest Passage proved unsuccessful, a trans-Alaskan pipeline was seen as the only economically viable method of delivering the crude to market. The richness of the Prudhoe Bay field also encouraged the oil companies to seek out other Arctic deposits.

The high costs of Arctic work forced the oil companies into special financial arrangements. Panarctic Oils, a consortium formed in 1967, was forty-five percent owned by the Canadian government and held exploration rights to forty-four million acres in the Arctic islands. A number of the major multinationals also rushed into the field, only to discover that expenses and risks were prohibitive, particularly in offshore exploration. Economic logic brought the competitors together to form Arctic Petroleum Operators Association. The consortium approach allowed the sharing of risks, and also profits, and permitted exploration to proceed where it otherwise would have stagnated.

Within the first three years of the 1970s, however, the face of the North American oil industry changed dramatically. The creation and toughening of the OPEC petroleum cartel, aided by an industry-fueled hysteria, touched off an international energy crisis. While motorists obligingly paid the escalating prices at the gas pump and national governments lectured about the need for energy self-sufficiency, the oil companies expanded drilling operations with Ottawa's blessings. The once-risky northern fields, proven and unproven, suddenly seemed unusually attractive.

The rapid surge in Arctic oil exploration did not go unnoticed by governments or interest groups. As early as 1968, the federal government had formed an inter-departmental Task Force on Northern Oil Development. As northern work expanded, and particularly as governments and industry learned, on the job, about the social and environmental risks associated with sub-Arctic and Arctic drilling, regulations were tightened and clarified. Anticipating the eventual need for a pipeline to connect northern reserves and southern markets, the government produced guidelines for pipeline construction in 1970 and revised these guidelines two years later.

Ottawa's attempts to regulate the frontier industry did not satisfy all the critics. Native peoples and organizations, particularly in the Mackenzie River Valley and Delta, were troubled by the lack of interest in and commitment to aboriginal needs and concerns. On the national front, many others were concerned about environmental questions and the regulation of frontier oil exploration. The establishment of the Canadian Arctic Resource Committee in 1971, a privately funded watchdog and one of the most professional lobbying agencies in the country, provided a different perspective on the questions surrounding the fast-track-ed development of northern petroleum reserves. CARC's persistent questioning about Arctic resource activities, echoed by the ecumenical church group Project North (formed in 1975) and a cacophony of northern, Native and environmental associations, convinced the government to toughen its regulations further and to keep a closer eye on the industry.

They had much to watch, for northern oil exploration expanded rapidly through the early 1970s. The Canadian Geological Survey estimated that the Mackenzie Delta-Beaufort Sea area held six billion barrels of oil and some ninety trillion cubic feet of gas, an assessment that was later moderated as more technical work was done. Such claims fueled investors' interest in the region, particularly when the federal government offered to pay a major portion of the cost of exploration.

Dome Petroleum, active in Arctic oil work from the early 1960s, continued to lead the way. With its fleet of drilling ships and ice breakers, Dome explored its own mineral leases in the Beaufort and Arctic islands. As the leader in Arctic exploration, particularly deep water work, Dome also discovered a ready market in drilling for other companies. Yet, despite handsome profits in some sectors of its operation, the company was beset with problems. Poor planning, a shocking lack of attention to the costs of exploration, and technological errors plagued Dome's Arctic ventures.

Dome was not alone in the North, although it was the major player. By 1976 Imperial Oil had drilled 150 wells in the region, spending over $500 million in the process. Esso, Shell, Texaco Gulf and Petro-Canada also had sizeable Arctic investments. While there were enough promising signs to encourage a continuation of the work — and enough federal incentives and tax-write-offs to pay most of the bills — discoveries in the Canadian Arctic were, at best, marginal. Still, Beaufort discoveries, the promise of additional finds and the prospect of delivering Prudhoe Bay natural gas to southern markets via a Canadian route combined in the midst of an era of mega-project mania to stimulate plans for a northern pipeline.

By the mid-1970s, three different companies were developing proposals for a Mackenzie Valley pipeline. Out of this initial competition emerged a single multi-national consortium, Canadian Arctic Gas Pipeline Ltd., which proposed one of the country's largest mega-projects ever, a pipeline from the Beaufort Sea to Alberta; from there, the existing North American pipeline grid would deliver the resource to American and Canadian markets. A connecting line would be built across the northern Yukon to Prudhoe Bay. On March 21, 1974, CAGPL filed a formal application with the National Energy Board for permission to start construction.

CAGPL would not have the field to itself for long. Bob Blair's upstart Foothills Pipe Lines of Calgary, pitching to the nationalist fervor of the Trudeau government, proposed an all-Canadian pipeline designed, unlike CAGPL's plan, to move Canadian gas to Canadian markets. As the application and investigation process unfolded, Foothills' proposal was altered several times to include an American branch and, in 1977, a route along the Alaska Highway to service the Alaskan fields.

The tendering of the CAGPL application led to the establishment of the Mackenzie Valley Pipeline Inquiry in March 1974. The government offered the head of the inquiry, Thomas Berger, little direction. He was to inquire into the social, environmental and economic impact of the proposed pipeline and to assess the technical merits of the company's plans. Starting in March 1975, he held the necessary formal hearings, plowing through mountains of technical data and analysis — much of it quickly found wanting — and listened to dozens of expert witnesses discuss the engineering questions associated with constructing and maintaining a pipeline that would stretch for hundreds of miles across the sub-Arctic. To the dismay of pipeline promoters, however, Berger also took his inquiry into thirty-five northern communities and listened to some 1000 witnesses.

Many developers, particularly in the oil industry, found much to fault in Berger's inquiry. His choice of advisors, including the controversial political economist Mel Watkins, they said, biased the investigation against their proposal. Others wondered aloud if the Native voices heard at the inquiry, consistently opposed to pipeline development, really spoke for all Northerners. The criticisms did not address the many concerns raised by the investigations. Berger had done what no previous inquiry had done: he listened to the Native people of the North, heard what they said and agreed with them. The startling consensus, and the unexpected passions in the Native community, surprised many

Canadians who followed the well-publicized Berger inquiry as it made its way around the North.

Few were surprised when Thomas Berger's report recommended that pipeline construction be put on hold for a decade, pending settlement of the Dene, Metis and Inuit land claims. But Berger was not alone in his reservations. The National Energy Board, holding hearings on the technical feasibility of the pipeline proposals, also found them wanting. Troubling environmental and engineering questions remained unanswered; the escalating costs of the pipeline construction also raised concerns. The NEB likewise rejected the CAGPL proposal and, instead, in July 1977 offered conditional support for Foothills' late entry into the pipeline sweep-stakes — the Alaska highway natural gas pipeline through the southern Yukon and northern British Columbia.

Even this project, however, could not proceed immediately. Another (and often ignored) inquiry, headed by Kenneth Lysyk, Dean of Law at the University of British Columbia, was given less than three months in the summer of 1977 to investigate the Foothills proposal. Meetings were held along the route of the planned pipeline, favoured by many because it ran along an existing development corridor. Like Berger, Lysyk recommended a delay in construction until land claims had been settled and called for strict environmental and social controls to limit the impact.

Although many technical questions remained only partially answered, the federal government decided to press ahead. In August 1977, an agreement in principle was signed with Foothills. Legislation was quickly implemented, including a federal Northern Pipeline Act and the Yukon's Northern Natural Gas Pipeline Ordinance. A complex deal was struck between the Canadian and American governments in 1977, removing one of the final hurdles to construction. The Canadian upstart had defeated a consortium of multi-national giants. The Mackenzie Valley proposals had been defeated but construction on the Alaska Highway route was slated to begin in 1981.

Along the highway route, communities and businesses braced for the economic explosion they felt was sure to accompany construction. In Whitehorse, targeted as construction head-quarters, signs of expansion could be seen throughout the town. But even as the official deals were being signed, there were indications of trouble in the offing. Initial estimates called for the construction of the pipeline for around $4.4 billion. As inflation soared and the natural gas market levelled off, costs escalated. By 1982, the estimate had more than tripled, to $15 billion. With North American banks rapidly turning sour on oil and gas development, an inevitable consequence of their incautious en-thusiasm for the oil patch in the 1970s, Foothills was forced to delay construction. In 1983, the company closed its Whitehorse office, a sure sign that the boom that never was had turned to bust. The suspension of pipeline construction plans was a cruel blow for a territorial economy already suffering from the malaise of a collapsing mining sector. While some hoped that the pipeline project would be re-started and others applauded the demise of what they viewed as an ill-conceived adventure, it was clear to all that the short-term infusion of pipeline construction invest-ment had been postponed indefinitely.

The cancellation of the pipeline project did not stop Arctic oil and gas exploration immediately. Panarctic, for example, con-tinued its work in the Arctic Islands and drilled successful wells on Cameron and Melville Islands. The company initially proposed the construction of a pipeline to southern markets, a concept that found little favour with environmental and Native groups across the country. In 1985, Panarctic dispatched a trial shipment of oil by tanker from its Arctic base to Montreal; the company is also involved in the Arctic Pilot Project, a similar plan to deliver liquified natural gas from the Arctic in ice-breaking tankers.

Despite occasional bursts of optimism, however, the overall picture of northern oil and gas development has fallen far short of the early promoters' vision. In the western district, Gulf Canada's promising Amauligak field, discovered in 1984 and originally estimated to hold 800 million barrels of oil, soon fell on hard times. Further work demonstrated that the initial reports had been overly optimistic. In addition, in the days of weakening federal support for Arctic exploration, high interest rates and declining world prices, the Arctic play lost much of its attractiveness.

Not all northern oil development followed the same convoluted path. Esso, owners of the Norman Wells oil field, decided in the 1980s to press ahead with further exploitation of the field. A $600-million expansion, built around six artificial islands and 160 additional wells, provided enough oil flow to justify the construction of a pipeline. By then, as well, the Canadian oil grid had reached Zama, Alberta, 900 kilometers to the south. Interprovincial Pipeline built a twelve-inch connecting line, completing the job in 1985. This pipeline project, carried out with considerable Native participation and without the rhetoric and fear of the previous decade, proceeded with little difficulty. Times clearly had changed.

For many in the oil patch, the problems with Arctic exploration and development lay with the Liberal government's controversial National Energy Program. Introduced in 1980, the legislation sought to ensure Canadian self-sufficiency in petroleum products within a decade while significantly increasing Canadian ownership in the industry. Majority Canadian ownership was required for companies wishing to receive new licences. The Petroleum Incentives Program (PIP) offered substantial grants (up to eighty percent of actual spending for wells drilled by companies at least seventy-five percent Canadian owned, and working in frontier areas) for exploration. The government also reserved for itself a controversial twenty-five percent share (the back-in provision) in any new oil and gas discoveries.

The major exploration companies, fearing the economic consequences of such measures, mounted a concerted attack on the program. There was a certain amount of posturing involved — market forces had already begun to dampen interest in frontier developments — but the removal of drilling rigs and the suspension of operations in the North by many companies sent shockwaves through the northern economy. The Liberals made some adjustments to the legislation in an attempt to attract the companies back, but they were turfed out of office by the Mulroney Conservatives before they had an opportunity to effect substantial changes. By the spring of 1985, the Conservative administration had suspended many of the provisions of the National Energy Policy, including the controversial Petroleum and Gas Revenue Tax and PIP grants. Alterations to the legislative framework were not enough, however, for low world prices continued to play havoc with exploration and development plans.

The impact of frontier oil exploration on the North is difficult to gauge. For a variety of political and economic reasons, northern oil has been viewed as a national and not a regional resource (as it is in Alberta). For this reason, the federal government typically justifies its investment in oil exploration and development in national terms — jobs created in the south, manufacturing spin-offs and the security of Canadian oil supply. Many of the oil patch workers, for example, live in the south, flying in on rotation as seasons and work schedules dictate. They are the ultimate transients, experiencing little of the North beyond their work-site and contributing even less to the economic, social and political life of the region.

Not surprisingly, the oil industry has had an uneasy relationship with the Native population, a tension highlighted by the radically different perspectives on the proposed Mackenzie Valley pipeline. Yet, while aboriginal people fear the possible environmental and social effects of oil exploration and development, the industry has begun to provide opportunities for Native participation.

It has not always been so. In the early days of the Beaufort Sea development, drilling crews and Native people in the Tuktoyaktuk region experienced considerable difficulties. Widespread abuse of alcohol and drugs, the large number of single young men brought in to work on the rigs and the social distance created by the provision of a few high-paying but low-skilled jobs for Inuit workers disrupted community life and soured relations between the Natives and Dome. The company did its best to control its workforce, moving its headquarters out of Tuk, limiting worker access to the settlement and trying to regulate the excesses of behaviour.

To improve communication between the Inuit and the company, Dome created the Beaufort Sea Community Advisory Committee, made up of representatives of seven communities. The committee was greeted with some cynicism — the representatives were accused of surrendering to Dome — and some anger, particularly among those who felt that the Inuit organization in the area, the Committee for Original Peoples' Entitlement, had been pre-empted by the new council. In time, however, the advisory committee began to make a substantial contribution, convincing Dome to respect Inuit ties to the land by providing time off for hunters, and providing a conduit for community concerns about resource development.

The disruptions of the transient, highly-paid frontier workforce continue to be felt in the North. While there have been efforts made to increase Native participation in the industry, with greater success than in the mining sector, the Inuit and Dene continue to suffer from a lack of marketable skills and from conflicting cultural expectations. In 1985, for example, when several mining companies were still active in the North, 5,587 individuals were employed. Of these, only 600 were Native people.

There are, however, indications that improvements are in the offing, aided by the negotiation and settlement of land claims. Esso's expansion of the Norman Wells field, while the object of some initial opposition from certain Native groups, nevertheless drew heavily on its partnership with Native enterprises, like Shehtah Drilling, owned and operated by Dene from nearby Fort Norman. The same has not been true of recent pipeline repair work, which has been contracted to an Edmonton firm. Equity investments and joint ventures carry certain risks of their own, tying community prosperity to the continued exploitation of non-renewable resources, but they do ensure Dene and Inuit people a greater say in the pace and direction of resource development, and a considerably more substantial share of the revenues being taken from their land.

Renewable Resources

The Native people have, of course, always taken sustenance from the land, but typically in the form of renewable resources. For centuries, carefully regulated hunting, fishing, trapping and harvesting provided the Dene and Inuit with the materials and foods they needed to survive. The arrival of European fur traders commercialized the harvesting of wild animals, altering the manner in which aboriginal people viewed the resources around them. Over the last two decades, following years of government efforts to bring the Natives off the land and into the mainstream of Canadian society, the aboriginal people have found their traditional uses of the land threatened.

On a grand economic scale, the harvesting of renewable resources seems to make only a marginal contribution to the North. Agriculture remains small in scale and largely experimental, limited by climate, high costs, soil types and, particularly in the Yukon, the difficulty in securing title to land pending a settlement of the land claim. There is some commercial fishing. In the Yukon, the Han Fishery out of Dawson City harvests salmon in the Yukon River. To the east, there are commercial fish plants in Hay River, Rankin Inlet and Cambridge Bay; their catch, marketed through the Freshwater Fish Marketing Board, capitalizes on gourmet interest in northern species. Similarly, northern forests have attracted some attention. But the relatively small amount of commercial-grade timber has little export value, and the few mills in the territory produce mainly for local use.

The single most important non-renewable sector is, surprisingly, not the fur trade but production of "country" food. In many Native communities, the land continues as a primary supplier of food. There are many reasons for this. Native people prefer the taste of country to store-bought food. They assign considerable cultural importance to the harvesting of animals and fish. The reliance on country food, which must be harvested when available, creates an interesting tension with wage labour, particularly when the standard North American work schedule is followed. Studies in Old Crow, Ross and Teslin in the Yukon documented that country food constitutes from forty to sixty percent of the food consumed in the community. If the dollar value of this food is calculated, it adds up to approximately $10 million a year (1985 figures) for the Yukon Territory. For many northern Natives, wage labour is primarily viewed as a means of securing the money and equipment necessary to continue hunting and trapping.

Country food production, despite its importance to the Native people, lacks the public profile of fur trapping. The harvesting for sale of fur bearing animals has been an integral part of Native life in the North since the 18th century, and continues to be a major source of income for Northerners. In 1986, northern trappers brought in over $4 million worth of furs, supporting more than 4,000 trappers in the Northwest Territories and 800 in the Yukon.

There are some important misconceptions about the northern fur trade, the first of which is that it is the main economic activity of Native people. In an extensive 1984 study of the "traditional" economy in the North, Jack Stabler identified the changing role of harvesting activities. Of more than 6,000 Native people employed in the Northwest Territories, only 1,200 were employed year round in traditional activities. Another 5,300 pursued harvesting activities on a seasonal basis. In addition, it was clear from Stabler's work that older Natives were far more likely than younger individuals to participate in harvesting activities.

The returns for trapping have also been less than lucrative, although it is important that trapping be recognized as only one part of a renewable resource harvesting cycle that includes hunting, fishing, gathering, occasional wage work and government transfer payments. In 1984-1985, for example, NWT trappers averaged only $870. Fewer than 1,200 earned more than $600 and only fifty had trapping incomes in excess of $8,000. Despite these modest economic returns — the social and cultural benefits of trapping cannot, of course, be readily quantified — there is great demand for trap-line space and very little room for expansion.

In the Northwest Territories, the Natives have the trapping field almost exclusively to themselves; to the west, in contrast, much of the trapping is done by non-Natives. In 1985, there were 768 licensed trappers in the Yukon Territory, including 314 non-

Natives, 302 status Indians and 152 non-status Natives. According to a recent government report, the non-Native trappers have been responsible for the largest share of furs taken in the territory over the last few years. There is nothing particularly new in this, for non-Native harvesters have been active in both the trapping and trading side of the industry for generations.

While the export of furs remains the foundation of the northern trade, greater attention has been paid of late to processing and using the resource in the North. Northern artisans have sold their handiwork on a casual basis for years, but little attention had been paid to the systematic development of the crafts. Aided by sizeable government grants, Native people in the Yukon created Yukon Native Products, an artists' co-operative, manufacturing centre and retail store. In the Northwest Territories, the community-based co-operatives have similarly been encouraging the production of clothing and art work using northern fur resources, garnering a greater share of the value of the fur trade for northern residents.

All this is now threatened. In the late 1960s, sparked by the controversy over the Newfoundland harp seal hunt, animal rights organizations launched a polemical campaign against the fur trade in general. Their self-righteous wrath knew few bounds, and demonstrated little real knowledge of the nature of the northern fur trade. This was not, of course, their concern. Animal rightists aimed to end what they viewed as cruel and inhumane treatment of animals. The claims of the Inuit, for example, that the protests were harming their subsistence-based economy were brushed aside. To Greenpeace activist Patrick Moore, the Inuit had aligned themselves with the exploiters of animal life; they had, he argued, been "co-opted into an unacceptable economy." Greenpeace would later recant, in part, and exempt Inuit hunters from their attacks. But for many Inuit communities, it was too late.

By the 1980s, the protest movement against the fur trade had expanded. The International League for Animal Rights, I KARE Wildlife Coalition, International Fund for Animal Welfare, Greenpeace International, Animal Defense League and other organizations, supported by a generation of urban North

Americans and Europeans whose lives had been almost totally divorced from experience of the land and its resources, united in a demand that the killing of fur-bearing animals be stopped. They pulled few punches. Graphic films, urban guerrilla tactics — such as spray-painting those who dared to wear a fur coat in public — and a well-orchestrated and emotion-laden political campaign proved very successful. The European Common Market, while stopping short of a total ban on the importation of seal skins, permitted individual countries to impose their own import restrictions.

The conflict between the animal rights organizations and northern harvesters is very basic. To the Natives and many non-Natives in the North, the harvesting of game for food or fur carries no particular moral dilemma. Hunting and trapping is an institutionalized way of life; as has been the case for centuries, game is killed to sustain life. For their opponents on the fur trade issue, the matter is just as simple: harvesting, particularly through the use of the leg-hold trap, which causes the trapped animal considerable pain and suffering, is immoral and in-humane. To such individuals, the alleged mistreatment of animals is an indication of a fundamental human failing. The two perspectives are at opposite poles, and it is difficult to imagine a compromise position.

The destruction of traditional markets has had an immediate effect in the North and has resulted in a sizeable loss of income. In Resolute, for example, sealing income dropped from almost $59,000 to $2400 in only two years in the early 1980s. Igloolik hunters received close to $46,000 for their seal skins one year, and around $5,000 two years later. In the Eastern Arctic, sealing was the backbone of the subsistence economy; the destruction of the market has led to a reduction in harvesting activities, a far greater reliance on government transfer payments and further alienation of the Inuit from their land.

Northern Indians are fighting back. Stephen Kakfwi, then President of the Dene Nation, commented in 1985 that the anti-trapping crusaders have their priorities misplaced:

> We understand that many people are worried about the loss of wildlife species throughout the world. We share this concern. But we also know that the greatest threat to animals is not from hunting and trapping. It is from the destruction of their natural habitat by the industrial society.... We believe we can offer our knowledge and experience as a people who live in close contact with nature to help change this dangerous trend.

The difference in this perspective from the anti-trapping lobby, whose uninitiated supporters recoil at the simple mention of the killing of a wild animal, is readily obvious. Making the protesters respect the opinions of the Natives is much more difficult. It does not, however, mean that northern Natives will readily surrender.

The cornerstone of the Native defence is Indigenous Survival International, an alliance of aboriginal peoples from Canada, Alaska and Greenland formed in Yellowknife in 1984. The organization is dedicated to preserving Native harvesting rights and to guaranteeing that fur and fur products continue to enjoy access to European markets. ISI is also determined that the Native perspective on harvesting and conservation be included in the scientifically dominated organizations pursuing a world conversation strategy.

The battle against the anti-fur trade lobby extends beyond Indigenous Survival International. The Yukon Territorial government has given financial support to the ISI, funded the Yukon Trappers' Association to prepare a film on northern trapping and assisted the Council of Yukon Indians to prepare an information booklet. The Northwest Territories legislative assembly has been similarly active, providing financial assistance, along with the Fur Institute of Canada and the federal government, for a major exhibit at the British Museum on the lifestyles of the Inuit, Metis and Dene. The northern campaign can claim a few successes. Greenpeace England was convinced to withdraw from a particularly aggressive group called Fur Free Britain; and Anglican and Catholic bishops from the North have issued statements in support of Native harvesting. Northern trappers have also changed their ways somewhat. With government encouragement, more and more trappers are switching to Conibear and other "humane" traps in response to the criticism of the leg-hold trap.

But the battle continues, and uncertainty remains. In the spring of 1988, British parliamentarians considered, and then turned down, a total ban on the importation of wild fur products into their country; Yukon politicians suggested only partially tongue-in-cheek a retaliatory ban on the importation of British products into the Territory. Indigenous Survival International is maintaining its efforts and met at Fort Yukon, Alaska, in June 1988 to co-ordinate the campaign to protect existing markets for northern pelts, stressing that the importance of the issue does not rest only with the potential for lost income; rather, the systematic and concerted attack on aboriginal subsistence harvesting represents a challenge to the very core of Native life.

Stephen Kakfwi is right, of course, and other northern leaders have echoed his observations. The synthetic substances touted by the anti-trapping forces as replacements for fur goods are created only at tremendous environmental cost. But those costs — the damage caused by mining, pollution, urban sprawl and the destruction of animal habitats — cannot be reduced to the simplistic images so attractive to the anti-trapping lobby. To the animal rights activists, northern Natives astride skidoos, bearing rifles and setting a few leg-hold traps, are seen as living anachronisms and are labelled a throw-back to a less humane time and culture. The fact that the Native people are much more attuned to their natural world, and more conscious of the need for careful conservation of renewable resources, is conveniently ignored. The battle will continue, for the anti-trapping lobbyists are not likely to surrender their position without many more well-financed campaigns. Native people, less well-funded, will also fight on, determined to gain respect for their lifestyle and to protect the markets for their trapping.

Trapping is not, of course, the only renewable resource option available to the North. In recent years, great importance has been placed on the development of the tourist trade, a relatively non-polluting, non-destructive, but potentially rich alternative to continued non-renewable resource exploitation. Divorced from the fluctuations of international commodity markets, it has the added benefit of protecting the northern economy from the inevitable booms and busts of the mining sector. In an age of increasing industrialization and urban concentration, the North is also discovering that what were once its greatest economic liabilities — isolation and wilderness expanses — have become its most important assets.

The Canadian government has recognized the uniqueness of its northern Territories. Three new national parks, Kluane in the Yukon, Auyuittuq and Nahanni in the Northwest Territories, were created in 1972. National park reserves (similar in status to national parks but subject to land claims negotiations) have been set up by the federal and territorial governments in the Northern Yukon and on Ellesmere Island. Although Native people and organizations generally favour the restrictions on non-renewable resource development, they are concerned about the implications of park designation for Native harvesting activities, and about the loss of control over these lands once they are designated as permanent parks. In the immediate term, however, the setting aside of park lands is a recognition of the unique environment in the North and of the need to protect these lands for future generations — of both Northerners and tourists.

The national parks have not yet been fully integrated into the North's tourism strategy. Nahanni's isolation has limited park use to a small number of travellers; Auyuittuq, a rugged wilderness of mountains, glaciers and fiords, is even more inaccessible, attracting only a few wilderness adventurers each year. Kluane, however, is a different matter. The park, initially set aside as a preserve in 1942 during construction of the Alaska Highway, has the highway as its western boundary. As a result, portions of the park are readily accessible to travellers. Parks Canada has, in recent years, expanded its program of activities at Kluane and has developed plans for roads and tours into the back-country glaciers. This proposal is sure to be greeted with considerable opposition from those who want the park, a UNESCO World Heritage Site, left untouched.

In the Northwest Territories, the exceptionally high travel costs limit the attractiveness for tourists. Economy fares to Yellowknife, Iqaluit or Inuvik run well over $1,000 from most southern centres; outlying communities, although well-served with scheduled and charter flights, are even more expensive to reach. Road access to the Liard and Mackenzie highways is limited; drivers must face long and gruelling journeys from southern centres. Still, travellers are venturing north in increasing numbers. In 1987, the Territories attracted 44,000 visitors; the industry supported over 200 tourist facilities of various descriptions and employed over 4,000 people on a full and part-time basis. Estimates call for steady growth over the next decade.

Tourists are attracted to the Northwest Territories by the call of the last great wilderness. A daunting array of hunting, fishing, canoeing, "flight-seeing" and other wilderness adventures satisfies the desire for a truly "northern" experience. For those with even more money and time, there have even been cruises through the Northwest Passage, the ultimate fantasy trip for the armchair explorer. Governments support these enterprises in a variety of ways. Arctic Hotline, a toll-free service for travel agents, provides access to a data bank on NWT opportunities. Travel Arctic, backed with a $2.3 million budget, provides a co-ordinated marketing campaign, targeted primarily at southerners and non-Canadians in search of a unique frontier experience. This kind of Territory-wide promotion allows the government to stress the significance of aboriginal culture and to encourage further development of related activities, like food production and northern handicrafts. Perhaps the best example of government-industry interdependence, however, was the NWT's extremely popular exhibit at Expo 86 in Vancouver, BC, the most important sign of the government's determination to expand tourism in the Territory.

If there is one concern about increased tourist interest in the North, it is that little of its profits would remain in the region. Organizations like Travel Keewatin have tried to counter this trend, urging the development of community-based tourism. Each community has been encouraged to develop tourist programs based on local opportunities and resources — arts and crafts tours to Eskimo Point, photography, hunting, fishing or wilderness adventures.

The tourist situation in the Yukon Territory is, not surprisingly, much different. Air rates are considerably lower, aided recently by the re-introduction of competitive service on the Whitehorse-Vancouver run. The Alaska Highway, upgraded substantially over the past two decades, provides ready automobile access to the territory. Improvements to the Stewart-Cassiar Road and Haines Road, the construction of the Skagway-Carcross highway and expanded service on the Alaska state ferry service have likewise made it easy for people to reach the Territory. The Yukon also offers travellers more options, including wilderness adventures, big-game hunting, river travels and historic tours.

The federal government has placed its greatest emphasis on the reconstruction of Dawson City. Since being designated as an historic site in the 1960s, the government has devoted millions of dollars to the preservation, rebuilding and interpretation of historic sites related to the Klondike gold rush. The effort starts, as the gold rush did, in Skagway, with the joint Canada-United States Chilkoot Pass Park. In Whitehorse, visitors can see the restored *S.S. Klondike*, rescued from the White Pass and Yukon Route shipyards, where its last remaining sister ships met a fiery death shortly after the *Klondike* was relocated. The government's priority, however, has long been Dawson City, where the Klondike Visitors' Association has fought to develop facilities suitable for tourists.

The Parks Canada attractions in the Dawson area host more than 65,000 visitors each summer. It is an expensive proposition. The 1987 budget called for an expenditure of $3.5 million per year on the historic sites in Dawson City, Bear Creek and Bonanza Creek. In Dawson City itself, Diamond Tooth Gertie's (a legal gambling saloon), the KVA's Palace Grand Theatre, Robert Service's cabin, the *S.S. Keno*, the Administration Building and other reconstructed buildings have been designed to recreate the ambiance of gold rush Dawson, and attract tourists to stay in the Yukon. Private enterprise has lagged behind the government's initiative; facilities are routinely jammed in the summer months, as campgrounds and hotels fill with tourists. Entrepreneurs are, however, finally beginning to jump on the gold rush bandwagon. The White Pass and Yukon Railway, closed in 1982, was re-opened in May 1988, running from Skagway to the Alaska-Canada border. A tour and freight riverboat service is scheduled to go into operation on the Yukon River in 1989, joining the many smaller operators offering summer tours between Whitehorse and Dawson City.

The effort is working. In the late 1970s, more than 300,000 tourists visited the territory every year. Expanded promotion, like the Yukon's Expo 86 pavilion, and special marketing efforts in Germany and the United States have been paying off. The number of people visiting the Yukon continues to grow steadily, filling the hotels, keeping tour operators, wilderness guides and other services busy during the short summer season. There remain, however, some troubling trends within the tourism sector. Few travellers have the Yukon as a final destination; most are simply passing through on their way to Alaska. Further, many are self-sufficient in their accommodations, travelling in campers and motor-homes. Considerable government and industry effort has therefore been devoted to keeping these people in the Territory a few extra days.

The Native Economy

The northern economy no longer rests on the simple mining-based foundations of the past. Yet the other sectors remain, in monetary terms, comparatively small, necessitating continued federal and territorial involvement to even out the bumps of the boom and bust cycles.

Ottawa, abandoning its inattention and neglect of earlier decades, has swamped the North with a kaleidoscope of economic development strategies and programs. Federal officials have directed particular attention to the development of a new Northern Mineral Policy, formally announced in December 1986. A complex series of economic deals with the territorial administrations, called Economic Development Agreements, provided local officials with large sums of money to encourage the diversification of the North's economic base. The territorial administrations have followed suit, undertaking construction projects, providing grants and setting local preference purchasing and contracting policies in an attempt to support regional business. These administrative initiatives have had mixed results. As the 1982-1985 depression in the Yukon Territory indicates, the region remains remarkably vulnerable to economic forces far beyond the North's control.

Non-Natives and Natives respond very differently to the economic forces that shape their lives. Many non-Natives, being immigrants to the region, simply leave when the mining economy or petroleum industry takes a sharp downturn. Native people, whose incomes are seldom directly tied to these major industries, do not perceive their options in the same manner. This being their homeland, they have not been willing to pick up and leave if economic times turn sour. For the past two decades, major efforts have been made, by the federal and territorial governments, to provide more opportunities for Native people.

The effort is not new. In the 1960s, considerable effort and money went into the creation and maintenance of retail and producer cooperatives in the Northwest Territories. Although the financial fortunes of the cooperatives have been mixed, the organizational experience and control that the system provide have been of major benefit to the Native people. Much more has been done recently. A number of Native development corporations, Native-owned and operated, have been opened across the North. The larger ones, Inuvialuit Development Corporation, Metis Development Corporation, Denendeh Development Corporation and Nunasi Corporation (central and eastern Arctic Inuit), represent the business interests of the major Native political organizations. The corporations allow Native people to be directly involved with the industries that affect their lives, provide on-the-job training and hold the potential for a profitable return.

Native people have established a formidable business presence in the North. The Nunasi Corporation, for example, has investments in Nunasi Central Airways (formerly Ontario Central), a Keewatin gold property, oil and gas holdings and publishing ventures. The Inuvialuit Development Corporation, founded in 1977 and holding many of the financial resources resulting from the COPE land claims settlement, had assets of $42 million in 1985. Investments included the Northern Transportation Company, Aklak Air, Madison Oil and Gas (Alberta), Bush Company (a local liquor store) and the Inuvialuit Petroleum Corporation.

Recent joint ventures reveal even more of the enormous changes that have swept through the North in the past fifteen years. Chevron Oil and the residents of Fort Good Hope, for example, have been working jointly on oil exploration in the area. The various projects employed 162 residents, including 129 from the local Native community. The Natives supplied heavy equipment, maintained the camps, provided contract labour and contracted for bush slashing and survey work. Chevron, for its part, paid for the work, provided training and some of the equipment and helped the development corporation establish new businesses.

Shehtah Drilling, established in 1983, represents a union of Esso Resources, Denendeh Development Corporation and the Metis Development Corporation. Ownership is split between the Native corporations and Esso, but is directed, managed and operated by the Natives. Shehtah Drilling, which provided thirty jobs (out of forty-five) for northern Natives on Norman Wells drilling projects in 1984, is designed to train Native people for work in the oil patch at both technical and managerial levels and to provide a solid financial return for investors.

The Cullaton Lake gold mine provides yet another example of Native and non-Native cooperative ventures. The Nunasi Development Corporation contributed a $27.9 million loan to the project, in return for the option to purchase shares. The cooperation went further, with forty of the 120 workers in the mine being Native. The Nunasi loan was repaid on schedule and the Inuit no longer have an equity share in the project, but their willingness to provide financial support has resulted in a far more favourable attitude toward the employment of Native workers.

Native business ventures have not all been in the non-renewable resource sector. Kal's Country Food, established in Rankin

Inlet in 1987, offered caribou meat, dried meat, seal and char,
purchasing the food from commercial hunters and offering it for
resale. Much has also been done to provide outlets for northern
artisans. The art cooperatives in the Northwest Territories, particularly the noted Cape Dorset and Baker Lake cooperatives,
have long promoted Inuit print-making and carving. Retail
operations such as Yukon Native Products and Northern Images
similarly promote Native handicrafts, serving as consignment
houses for people wishing to market their work. Many other
operations across the North — construction companies, airline
companies, retail stores, producers' cooperatives, guiding and
tour companies — are owned and operated by Native people.
An increasing number of these enterprises are community-
owned and based, a marked departure from the individualistic
and entrepreneurial model of the non-Native business community, but in keeping with the needs and aspirations of the
Native people of the North.

Even with these developments, however, Native businesses
form only a small percentage of the northern commercial sector.
In 1986, for example, only fifty-five of 1378 businesses in the
Yukon were Native-owned or run. Also, many Native business
activities carry an implicit commitment to non-renewable
resource development, which may be at odds with other Native
aspirations, such as the preservation of traditional lifestyles. Still,
Native corporations permit the Indian, Metis and Inuit communities to capture a greater share of the financial benefits from
the northern economy, to gain the professional, technical and
managerial skills needed in an increasingly complex society and
to provide employment for Native people in the North.

New Directions

Economic diversification remains a central, if elusive, goal for
northern politicians and businessmen, holding the potential of
freeing the region from the inevitable and disastrous boom and
bust cycles of the past. Recognizing the problems inherent in a
resource-based economy, the Yukon NDP government, first
elected in 1985, announced a bold planning initiative.

The "Yukon 2000" process sought to involve all Yukoners in a systematic evaluation of the territorial economy, with the hope that the planning process would indicate (or create) a consensus on the best path for the Yukon. The process started in Faro in June 1986, with a small gathering of representatives from various territorial associations and interest groups. From the Faro launch, the process expanded rapidly, through a series of public meetings, seminars and consultations. The effort was remarkably wide-ranging. All sectors of Yukon society were well represented: Natives, women, mining, tourism, organized labour, youth, handicapped, trappers and hunters, volunteer groups, local governments, seniors, public servants and many others. The planning process identified the major sectors of the economy and the significant economic links that tied the Yukon together.

The government was taking a considerable risk in asking such a diverse group to discuss such a controversial and wide-ranging issue. As the Yukon 2000 process continued, however, it seemed to gain momentum. A major conference was held in Whitehorse in the fall of 1986. As a result of this meeting and further consultations, the government produced *The Things That Matter: A Report of Yukoners' Views on the Future of Their Economy and Society* in August 1987, the document listing dozens of the recommendations offered at the discussions as solutions to the Yukon's problems.

The Yukon 2000 process did not produce quick answers or even a strong consensus on plans for the future. However, the discussions did demonstrate that the distance between the various interest groups was not as great as many had long expected. Many observers were attracted to the unique exercise. Peter McDowell, a business professor at the University of Alaska, commented, "This government appears to be sensitive, intelligent, and dynamic for economic leadership, and this should be a model for an Alaska regional development strategy. I find Yukon 2000 to be a charismatic process to which I am keenly attracted." Tony Penikett, Yukon government leader, offered a solid rationale for the undertaking:

> We are saying, here is an exercise in which, for the first time, you as a citizen or businessman or trade union leader or Indian band leader will have the chance to have a continuing voice in the kind of economy you want to see developed, and how we can do it. The most successful societies in the world are ones that share common goals and assumptions about where they want to go and how they want to get there.

The Yukon 2000 process is not yet complete, and it will be several years before direct benefits can be seen from the complex and involved discussions. But the significance of the process rests not with short-term results, but with the effort itself. The willingness of the territorial government and dozens of its most active and informed citizens to step outside their normal activities in order to contemplate the future of their Territory indicates a commitment to the region — and to a sustainable, stable economy — that has long been missing in the Canadian North.

Looking Ahead

Much has changed in the northern economy over the last fifteen years. The pipeline projects, touted as the foundation for growth and prosperity, withered and died, the massive reports and proposals that accompanied them remaining as testimony to misplaced dreams and aspirations. Mining is still the cornerstone of the regional order, with a marked shift to precious metal production following the collapse of base metal prices in the early 1980s. Around the fringes, and moving ever closer to centre-stage, are the smaller sectors — tourism, renewable resource development, services and secondary processing — that hold the opportunity for a balanced and stable regional economy. Although the statistics clearly indicate that Native people (particularly those with little or no formal education) remain outside the economic mainstream, there are also promising signs of Native participation, both as workers and as owners, throughout the North. Regional prosperity is no longer exclusively reserved for the largely transient, non-Native population.

Behind it all, and providing the essential financial props that preserve prosperity, are massive federal and territorial expenditures. The hand of government is everywhere to be seen — in interventionist petroleum legislation, grants to Native organizations and corporations, transportation or supply subsidies and major investments in infrastructure. As Native organizations and territorial governments take a larger role in the economic decision-making process, it is also clear that federal expenditures are having a greater impact. While it is too soon to argue that large mining projects, like Cyprus-Anvil or Pine Point, no longer dominate economic planning in the North, it is obvious that Northerners have set new priorities for the future development of their region.

Will the North achieve the economic stability and diversification it seeks? The answer remains unclear. The colonies are now fighting back, determined to capture a greater share of regional resources and income for the North and to upset the long-established model of northern development. Southern corporations and the federal government move more cautiously now that they did fifteen years ago in developing the North's resources, and listen with respect to the wishes of the northern communities. As the people of the region take a bigger role in planning and implementing their own economic agenda in the Yukon and Northwest Territories, there is much greater chance that the age-old pattern of boom and bust, of reliance on transient southern workers and of the marginalization of the North's aboriginal citizens, will give way to a more promising course.

3

Political Cultures: The Reality of Colonial Status

The most public battle against Canadian colonialism is being waged on the political front. Over the past fifteen years, the Yukon and Northwest Territories have argued for greater political autonomy and greater control over their own affairs. The political structures and arrangements that govern the North have, as a consequence, been modernized and, to a substantial degree, transferred to the region. Yet the transition is far from complete, as the controversy over the Meech Lake constitutional accord demonstrates only too well. Even as the North moves towards political equality and maturity, there is considerable evidence that colonialism will not disappear easily.

The Ottawa Scene

Since World War II, the greatest political challenge facing the North has been the struggle for recognition. The Yukon and Northwest Territories typically have had a minor place in the national scheme of things, attracting little attention from federal politicians and civil servants. Not since the days of John Diefenbaker, when northern development was offered as a "New National Policy," has the region sat near the top of the federal government's agenda. As a result, northern politicians have struggled, with only limited success, to focus attention on regional concerns and to heighten national interest in northern affairs.

The North's representatives to the federal House of Commons bear primary responsibility for carrying the North's message to the other members of parliament. The Yukon has been electing men and women to the House of Commons since 1901; the Northwest Territories did not receive a separate seat in Ottawa until 1952. For much of this century, the region's representatives have enjoyed only limited success in raising the profile of territorial concerns. Like the region they represented, most northern MPs faded into the background.

The Yukon's Erik Nielsen broke this pattern. First elected in a December 1957 by-election and a back-bencher during the years of Conservative rule, Nielsen emerged as an important political figure during the 1960s. A World War II veteran, and a man noted for his grit, loyalty, partisanship and determination, Nielsen was something of a muckraker, noted for bringing news of Liberal scandals to public attention. More important, he rose regularly in the House of Commons to press territorial concerns, offering a particularly persistent appeal for provincial status for the Yukon. Nielsen represented well the interests of the business community, and urged the rapid development of territorial resources, but he never neglected the rest of his Yukon constituency. He earned his support the hard way, through careful attention to constituency affairs and to an unwavering defence of territorial interests in Ottawa.

Nielsen represented the Yukon for thirty years, winning ten more elections in the process, before retiring in January 1987. While his string of electoral victories was unbroken, it would be wrong to assume that all Yukoners were pleased with his leadership or his party. In the 1968 election, for example, Liberal candidate Chris Finlay rode Trudeaumania to within sixty-two votes of the long-serving incumbent. Following his re-election in 1979, Nielsen was appointed minister of public works in Joe Clark's short-lived Conservative administration. The position was an important one for the North; a temporary burst in funding for the reconstruction of the Alaska Highway was one of the more important legacies of his brief tenure in the minister's chair.

Although there were signs that Nielsen was tiring of federal politics, he stayed on. He barely held his seat in a tight 1980 electoral battle, but emerged as one of the most prominent figures in the federal Conservative caucus. He stood behind Joe Clark when the leader faced, and lost, a leadership challenge. It was a sign of Nielsen's high reputation within Conservative ranks that one of the first things that Brian Mulroney did upon unseating Clark as Conservative leader was to appoint Nielsen as deputy leader. In the Conservative sweep of 1984, the Yukon seat remained Tory blue, with Nielsen winning by more than 4,000 votes.

Nielsen's loyalty and prominence assured him a major role in the Mulroney government. As deputy prime minister, he performed as one of the administration's most important troubleshooters. He chaired a major and controversial task force on government spending and programs, a study group that had official Ottawa trembling for months on end, and replaced Robert Coates when the latter was forced to resign his post as minister of national defence. The positions gave Nielsen an unexpected national presence, but he did not ignore the North. In May 1985, he announced an $8.7 million economic development grant for his home territory and a new financing agreement which increased the Yukon's capital budget from $27 million to $42 million.

Yet, while no one questioned Nielsen's loyalty to the prime minister and his administration, he was to become a political liability. The political characteristics that had served Nielsen so well in opposition — his partisanship, tenacity and combativeness — did not transfer easily to the government benches. "Velcro Lips," so named for keeping information (including news of his re-marriage) under close control, became a favourite opposition target. In January 1987, the political wars having taken their toll, Nielsen announced his resignation. In typical fashion, he offered few comments on his departure — not even to the party faithful in the North— and retreated to his lodge on Quiet Lake. But he did not disappear completely from public life, accepting an appointment to the Canadian Transport Commission.

The 1987 Yukon by-election campaign triggered by Nielsen's resignation was a three-sided contest, fought by Audrey McLaughlin of the New Democrats, Tory candidate David Leverton, a relative newcomer to Yukon politics, and popular Whitehorse mayor Don Branigan of the Liberals. The battle focused on the Yukon's opposition to the Meech Lake constitutional deal; it was clear from early in the competition that Leverton would feel the brunt of territorial anger at the Mulroney government. While Nielsen, interestingly, was conspicuous by his absence from the by-election, the territorial NDP turned its considerable electoral team into their candidate's campaign. McLaughlin, a social worker by training, won, earning 332 more votes than Branigan. Leverton finished third, a sure mark of the end of the Nielsen dynasty. While McLaughlin had little time to establish a national presence, she broke with her leader and party on the Meech Lake deal. She has also been much more outspoken on northern issues, particularly constitutional matters and Native affairs, than was the close-lipped Nielsen.

No other northern representative in Ottawa has risen to Nielsen's stature. For much of the post-war period, a single member of parliament represented the entire Northwest Territories, a daunting and tiring political task. Wally Firth, a Native rights worker and commercial pilot, carried the Northwest Territories for the New Democratic Party in 1972 and won again in 1974. Before the 1979 election, the Northwest Territories was divided into two electoral districts. In Nunatsiaq (Eastern Arctic), Peter Ittinuar of the NDP defeated the prominent Native activist Tagak Curley of the Liberal Party. In the west, mining engineer Dave Nickerson of the Progressive Conservatives won a close three-way race. Both men ran again the following year, and each eked out a narrow victory: Nickerson by nineteen votes over Wally Firth and Ittinuar by 311 ballots over Liberal James Arvaluk.

Neither Ittinuar or Nickerson, however, established much of a presence in Ottawa. Both men, in fact, became embroiled in personal difficulties that distracted them from their constituency work. Nickerson, a pro-development advocate and former territorial cabinet minister, had represented his Mackenzie region well, as demonstrated by a sizeable victory over the Liberals and NDP in the 1984 election. But a well-publicized domestic dispute, which resulted in opposition party demands that Nickerson resign his seat, tarnished his image and temporarily reduced his effectiveness.

Peter Ittinuar's career has followed an even more tortuous path. The former CBC announcer, film-maker, magazine editor, executive member of the Inuit Tapirisat, and professor of Inuktituk linguistics and culture, crossed the floor to the Liberals in 1982. His once-promising career soon lay in tatters, demolished by unproven accusations concerning the use of government funds. But Ittinuar was not about to give up. He ignored the many signs of his growing unpopularity, including the loss of the NDP nomination in the 1984 nomination. Running as an independent, he received only ten percent of the votes cast and finished well behind the winner, Thomas Sulak of the Progressive Conservatives.

The November 1988 federal election saw further political change in the NWT and a confirmation of the decision taken a year earlier in the Yukon. Audrey McLaughlin (now NDP caucus chairperson and widely touted as a potential leadership candidate) won handily, confirming that the by-election victory of 1987 had been no fluke. McLaughlin won, in part, because of her strong opposition to the Meech Lake Accord and excellent constituency work. In the NWT, voters bucked the national trend, rejecting incumbent Tory MP Dave Nickerson in the Western Arctic and sending two Liberals, Ethel Blondin (Western Arctic) and Jack Iyerak Anawak (Nunatsinq), to Ottawa.

The federal political forum has proven to be of marginal value for Northerners. Regional members of parliament have seldom been able to bring northern issues to the attention of the House of Commons, beyond routine private members' motions that attract little notice. Partly because of the limited ability of individual MPs to affect the nation's political agenda and partly because there is so much work to be done at the territorial level, much of the region's political energy has been devoted to the unique and innovative territorial administrations.

Politics in the Yukon

The Yukon has had a long history of political representation at the territorial level. In 1908, an amendment to the Yukon Act established a fully-elected ten-member territorial council, although the political power of the commissioner — the federally appointed head of government — limited that body's real power. In 1918, in the wake of a massive cut in territorial appropriations, the council was reduced to three elected members. Improvements to the territorial political scene came only after World War II.

Through the 1960s, Yukon politics was noted for its raucous character. Controversial and outspoken members like Ken Mackinnon, Norm Chamberlist, Hilda Watson, Clive Tanner and Jim Howett guaranteed lively and rich debate. The often confrontational atmosphere originated, at least in part, in the absence of substantial power in the hands of the territorial representatives. Anxious for greater authority, the Yukon Territorial Council introduced an autonomy motion in 1966, calling for an elected council of fifteen members, provincial status within twelve years and the creation of an executive committee with full cabinet powers. The federal cabinet countered in 1967 with a demand that the Yukon raise a greater share of territorial revenues. When the Territorial Council refused, Ottawa temporarily cut off federal grants.

And then, slowly, real change began. With Yukoner James Smith as commissioner, some major alterations were made to the structure and administration of government. In November 1970, two elected members, Hilda Watson and Norm Chamberlist, were appointed to the five-member Executive Council which, with the commissioner, served as the territorial cabinet. Four years later, another elected representative was added to the council. Three years later, in 1977, the addition of yet another member gave elected officials a majority. Party politics formally arrived in 1978, when the Progressive Conservatives won eleven of the sixteen seats on Council. In the following year, 1979, the first fully elected cabinet was sworn in under Government Leader Chris Pearson. Responsible government had arrived.

For the Conservative administration, control of the Executive Council was not enough. Chris Pearson wrote to Jake Epp, Minister of Indian Affairs and Northern Development:

> The growth of the Executive Committee concept and the advent of party politics to the Yukon legislature have made it possible to entrust a large portion of the responsibility for the active, day to day administration of the Yukon government to elected officials directly accountable to the Yukon Legislative Assembly. In this context, it is our contention that the Commissioner need not and should not continue to play a prominent role in the day to day administration of the Yukon government.

The challenge to the commissioner's position was not unexpected. The appointment of Art Pearson in 1976 was particularly unpopular, and his resignation under a cloud in 1978 did a great deal to diminish the prestige of the position. The appointment of popular and influential Yukoner Ione Christensen in January 1979 was greeted much more enthusiastically, but the political groundswell against the power of appointed officials had gained too much momentum. Minister Jake Epp accepted the Yukon's position and advised Christensen that the commissioner would no longer sit on the Executive Committee and was to accept the advice of elected council on all matters. The commissioner was, in Epp's words, to be a "mediator in the constitutional development of the Yukon." Christensen was not comfortable with the diminished status, and resigned her office in "protest against the Territory's pell mell dash towards democracy." She ran unsuccessfully against Erik Nielsen in the 1980 federal election campaign.

The Yukon was not, of course, content with the achievement of responsible government. Since the 1960s, some Yukoners had demanded provincial status. Enthusiasm for the idea had never been widespread, but it did enjoy considerable support among Conservative followers. The Yukon plan received a major boost with the selection of Joe Clark as federal Progressive Conservative leader. Shortly after becoming leader of the Official Opposition, Clark visited the Territory and, backed by Erik Nielsen, promised that the Yukon would move towards provincial status during the Conservatives' first term of office. To Clark's dismay, the offer was greeted with considerable scepticism and limited enthusiasm. As residents looked carefully at the financial cost of such status, their support dimmed markedly.

Yet, while many Yukoners recognized that becoming a province was not in their immediate interest, there was a desire to continue the process of constitutional reform and to ensure that the option of future change would remain open. Ironically, as the Yukon moved towards greater local control over its affairs, Yukoners discovered that their political future was becoming increasingly constrained. When Prime Minister Trudeau, back in office after 1980, was asked about the prospect of provincial status for the Yukon, he bluntly replied, "Not in my lifetime." In 1980 Chris Pearson demanded an invitation to the First Ministers' Conference on the Constitution; he was refused. Further, territorial demands for control over lands and resources, fueled by the Native land-claims process, were repeatedly rejected.

The debate over constitutional reform was not over — a host of unresolved problems kept the issue alive. Even with the changes of the 1970s, the Yukon had far fewer powers than the provinces, particularly in the crucial area of land and resources. It lacked the ability to amend its own constitution and faced the prospect of continued federal control over territorial legislation. Finally, Ottawa retained considerable power over Yukon financial matters, necessitating continual negotiations between territorial and federal officials over territorial funding.

Yet the broad strokes of constitutional change do not tell the entire story. The 1970s and early 1980s witnessed considerable progress in the area of administrative decentralization. Beginning in 1971, when the Yukon government acquired control over the administration of justice, a number of federal responsibilities were turned over to territorial officials. Public Works Canada handed the Alaska Highway to the Yukon Department of Highways in 1972. The same year partial responsibility for local fisheries was transferred to the Yukon government. The transfer of health care took longer, slowed by Native concerns and a lack of funds, but the territorial administration made significant gains in this area as well.

The transition was not always smooth, slowed by the territorial government's limited financial resources. Discussions started in the 1970s over the need for a formula financial agreement for the Territory, but a deal was not reached until 1985 (a second agreement has recently been ratified). The process of devolution, the North's principal option given the rejection of provincial status for the Yukon, has continued through the 1980s. The federal government clearly supports the ongoing transfer of administrative responsibilities, although the generosity has stopped short of offering the Yukon control over natural resources.

The territorial government's acquisition of greater powers occurred simultaneously with the emergence of political parties. For many in the Yukon, the introduction of parties was a sign of the Territory's political maturation. Through the 1960s, territorial legislators had avoided overtly partisan politics, although the federal affiliations of most politicians were well known. In the 1974 territorial election, the New Democratic Party agreed to identify its party candidates; the Progressive Conservatives, adhering to a national party policy that required a field of fifteen candidates before a party slate would be offered to the electorate, declined to run as a group. As long-time Tory Ken McKinnon argued, "the party shouldn't split the Yukon with partisan politics."

In the 1978 election, the first run completely along party lines, the Tories swept to power, winning eleven of the sixteen seats. These were not, however, elections that the rest of the country would immediately recognize; they were more like small-town municipal campaigns than provincial elections. In the smaller ridings, fewer than three hundred people went to the polls. Conservative Howard Tracy, for example, won the Tatchun constituency with 109 votes, twenty-six votes ahead of his nearest challenger. In Old Crow, winner Grafton Njootli gained sixty-two votes, more than twice the number of Liberal challenger

Ethel Tizya. Not all the ridings had so few voters — the Whitehorse constituencies were substantially larger — but these were clearly small-scale elections, fought on a local level, and with political personalities and local reputation playing a determining role in the contests.

The Conservatives seemed secure in their control of territorial political life, backing Erik Nielsen at the national level and returning a Tory majority to the Territorial Council. The 1982 election, fought primarily between the Tories and the NDP, reflected a certain polarization of territorial politics. The NDP, strong supporters of the Council of Yukon Indians' land claim, made significant inroads in the rural constituencies. The pro-development Tories held most of the Whitehorse ridings. When the dust had settled, the Conservatives had won again, holding nine of the sixteen seats and leaving the NDP with six seats.

The Progressive Conservatives offered a strongly ideological administration. There was a series of struggles over Native land claims, with the territorial government demanding attention to the need for a settlement of the Yukon's claim to control over land and resources. The Yukon Territorial Government pulled out of the land claims negotiations in 1982, returning reluctantly the following year. Determined efforts were also made to create a favourable atmosphere for investment in the Yukon. The government's support for short-term development, and the absence of a long-term plan for the diversification of the territorial economy, suggested that the Conservatives accepted the long-established economic pattern in the region.

While the Tories rode the wave of economic prosperity through the 1970s, they faced the consequences of their commitment to resource development following the economic collapse of the early 1980s. The recession forced cuts in legislators' wages, restrictions on government employees' pay and a reduction in work schedules. But the Tories' problems ran deeper than this. In the early 1980s, the Pearson government lost four ministers to scandals and personal problems. Pearson himself resigned in 1985, and soon afterwards he received a patronage appointment from the federal government as the federal representative in Dallas, Texas. Willard Phelps, whose family's ties in the Territory go back to the days of the Klondike gold rush, was selected to replace Pearson, a choice that was not uniformly popular throughout the Territory.

Phelp's first challenge, and a major test for the Tories' pro-development philosophy, came in the 1985 general election. The NDP, led by Tony Penikett and with strong support in the Native communities, offered a clear alternative to the Conservative Party. The election was a true Yukon barn-burner. The once-substantial Faro riding, for example, had been significantly depleted by the closure of the Cyprus-Anvil mine. Liberal Jim McLachlan won with only 142 votes. In Watson Lake, a battle within Conservative ranks resulted in two independent candidates running, in addition to the official PC representative. The conflict allowed NDP member David Porter to sneak into office. It was a tight battle throughout the Territory — the Tories actually won more votes than the NDP — but a distribution of seats in favour of the rural areas gave the NDP a minority government. The two Liberals held the balance of power.

The uncertainty would not linger long. Liberal leader Roger Coles ran into difficulties when he attempted to sell cocaine to an undercover RCMP officer. Coles resigned the leadership and, when found guilty of trafficking, also gave up his Tatchun seat. A by-election was called, with local Native Danny Joe running for the NDP against a prominent Liberal, Indian activist Elijah Smith. Joe won the contest, giving the NDP nine out of the sixteen seats in the territorial assembly.

Even before the Tatchun victory, Tony Penikett had launched a program to revitalize the Yukon. Working quickly to placate the business interests who were worried about the NDP's apparent unwillingness to support mining development, the government successfully negotiated the re-opening of the Faro mine. The government was also committed to the diversification of the territorial economy, and sponsored the Yukon 2000 consultation process in an attempt to seek guidance and, they hoped, a consensus on future directions. To speed up the land-claims process and to reassure its Native supporters, the NDP appointed former judge Barry Stewart as chief territorial negotiator. Perhaps most important, the new administration revitalized the

Territory's large and influential civil service, a group that had grown rather moribund and somewhat gun-shy under the reign of Tory free-enterprisers.

A territorial general election in February 1989 provided the first major test of the Penikett government. The usual territorial dynamics entered into the race — a moribund Liberal party struggling for respectability, unusual nominating meetings and a string of personality-based campaigns. The NDP were returned to power, winning nine of the sixteen seats. The Conservatives, led by Willard Phelps, won the remaining seven ridings. The Liberals ran close to a full slate of candidates but were shut out; the party finished third in all but one riding.

The electoral victory confirms that NDP policies have been popular of late. The Conservative Party remains an important, if weakened, force in territorial politics. The Liberals, on the other hand, seem destined for perennial third-party status, clearly without a sizeable territorial following. There have, therefore, been two significant shifts in territorial politics in the Yukon over the last fifteen years: the introduction of party politics and the replacement of Tory domination with NDP supremacy.

Politics in the Northwest Territories

These same forces of change have likewise swept through the Northwest Territories, although the timing and consequences of constitutional reform in that region have differed significantly from the situation in the Yukon. The two Territories started from the same base — colonies of a distant and often uncaring federal government — but the Northwest Territories' advance towards responsible administration has been much slower. For most of the century, until the mid-1960s, the territorial government was based in Ottawa. The council consisted of federal civil servants until after World War II, when local residents were finally appointed. Having regional representatives helped somewhat, but with the capital still located in Ottawa, residents had little say in the governance of their land.

Pressured by regional demands for greater autonomy, the federal government finally acted. In 1963, Ottawa appointed an

Advisory Commission on the Development of Government in the Northwest Territories, under the leadership of A.W.R. Carrothers, dean of law at the University of Western Ontario. The Carrothers Report, tabled in October 1966, recommended that, over time, the powers of the elected officials be increased and the authority of the appointed commissioner be reduced. A number of people had proposed the division of the Territories; the Carrothers commission advised postponing such a division, arguing that it would retard the progress of the NWT towards local autonomy.

The changes did not come immediately. By 1970, the fourteen-member territorial council consisted of ten elected and four appointed officials. In 1974, the NWT Act was amended, providing for a fully elected fifteen-member council. The face of northern politics changed in other ways. In the 1975 territorial elections, nine of the fifteen members were of Native descent, the first time that aboriginal people had ever held a majority in a democratically elected assembly in Canada. In 1979, the council was expanded to twenty-two members; fourteen of the elected members were of Native ancestry.

There is far more to the Territories' political system than its ethnic balance. The territorial system operates on an unusual non-partisan, consensual format that offers no assurance of assembly support for government measures and requires all politicians to seek a moderate, widely acceptable course. Territorial counsellors are elected on the basis of their stature within the community, not their party affiliation. Several members have been elected by acclamation since 1970. Government leaders, to provide a further example of consensus in operation, do not represent a stable voting block in the assembly and do not assume office solely on the basis of territorial election results. Rather, the leader is selected by elected representatives from among their own number. The leadership has rotated — from Richard Nerysoo to Nick Sibbeston to Dennis Patterson between 1985 and 1988 — without the incumbent being defeated in the house or losing his seat in the assembly. The process, which draws on the Natives' tradition of consensual governance, protects against the concentration of power, helps limit the likelihood of excessive patronage and, as with the selection of cabinet ministers, provides an effective check on political leaders.

The political career of Tagak Curley illustrates the effectiveness of the consensus format. An Inuk born in Coral Harbour, Curley worked his way up the ranks of Inuit politics and community organizations. After stints with the federal and territorial governments, he served as settlement manager at Repulse Bay. He was a founding member and first president of the Inuit Tapirisat and president of the Nunasi Development Corporation. He was first elected to the NWT council in 1979, representing Keewatin South and, later, Aivilik. In 1984, Curley was appointed Minister for Economic Development and Tourism, with additional responsibility for Energy, Mines and Resources and the Public Utilities Board. In his ministerial capacity, he served on a variety of committees and coordinated the NWT's highly successful exhibit at Expo 86 in Vancouver.

But at this point, Curley's political career, which demonstrates the close connection between local organizations, government service, Native politics and territorial affairs, was almost over. In 1987 he was accused of threatening a member of the territorial assembly over questions of grants to private businesses in the minister's riding. The legislative assembly voted to strip him of his ministerial position. He subsequently lost his seat in the October 1987 election, ending in ignominious fashion (perhaps temporarily) a distinguished political career. Tagak Curley's removal demonstrates the ability, and willingness, of territorial counsellors, operating under the consensus system, to take quick, tough and painful decisions, freed from the constraints of partisan politics.

The system has not rested unchallenged. As early as 1979, the New Democratic Party declared its intention to introduce party politics into the Territory. While the proposal found some supporters — some said such a transition was inevitable as the North modernized — the concept foundered. Yellowknife South MLA Lynda Sorensen attempted to organize a "Northern Party" in 1983; both the Liberal and Conservative parties rebuffed her suggestions.

There have been many critics of the consensus system. Political scientist Michael Wittington has argued that the "problem with the system is that there is no collective responsibility in the executive.... Without some collective responsibility to the legislature, it is impossible to have responsible government in the conventional sense." The NWT Chamber of Commerce declared that party politics would offer better accountability and would permit long-range planning. Others have favoured the introduction of new political parties, created in and for the North, rather than importing them from the south. (Regional voting patterns evident in the assembly suggest that this process is already underway, if informally.) But there are also many people, especially among Natives and in the Eastern Arctic, who find the consensus format to be less divisive and less confrontational than the party system, and fear that partisan politics could endanger land-claims negotiations and movement towards division of the NWT.

The evolution of the territorial political system continues. In the spring of 1988, a committee of ordinary members — the fifteen members of the Legislative Assembly who do not sit in cabinet — was formed. The committee assumed the role of an official opposition, bombarding cabinet ministers with questions and forcing them to justify major decisions publicly. Government Leader D. Patterson contends that this latest wrinkle does not represent an end to consensus government, pointing out the government would have quickly toppled had the committee of ordinary members been functioning as a true opposition party. The evolutionary process will undoubtedly continue, as the Northwest Territories struggles towards a stable political course that seeks to blend national political structures and traditions with the realities of territorial life. Importantly, NWT politicians have learned to approach southern political models with scepticism; they are determined that political change will continue at the North's pace and according to the region's agenda.

Within this uniquely northern and Native political system, territorial legislators have pushed steadily for an expansion of constitutional and administrative powers. In the mid-1970s, the NWT government proposed a full-scale reassessment of its status within confederation, but the federal government moved on its own. Former Liberal cabinet minister Bud Drury was appointed in 1977 to a commission on constitutional development. He was instructed to pay particular attention to Native proposals for new government structures.

The NWT legislative assembly did not wait for Drury's report. In March 1979, the assembly unanimously endorsed a demand for immediate responsible government with continued evolution towards provincial status. Further demands called for the removal of appointed officials, including the commissioner, and devolution of government activities to the communities.

The Drury Report, submitted in 1980, identified some fundamental flaws in the NWT's political structures. The report suggested that Native concerns were not well handled within existing arrangements. Drury also argued that the potential of local government had not been fully realized. He commented, "local government can provide for a measure of the self-government which Native people seek, but within the framework of a single territorial government. This would avoid an ethnically differentiated arrangements, which is anathema to Ottawa." The report recommended much greater emphasis on local government than was common in the south, and argued that many areas of federal responsibility should be transferred to the territorial government.

The Drury Report echoed, rather than stimulated, territorial demands for political reform. There was a practical side to this political re-structuring. The Northwest Territories Council moved to make the Executive Council more truly responsible. In 1980, George Braden, MLA from Yellowknife North, was selected by fellow councillors as the first leader of an elected executive. Thomas Butters became the first elected territorial minister of finance in 1980. (Two additional members were added to the Executive Committee in 1981.) Butters instigated a major shift in financial structures, removing federal control of territorial funding and negotiating a formula financing arrangement similar to the relationship between Ottawa and the provinces.

Territorial politicians kept the pressure on, negotiating with Ottawa for the continued transfer of federal responsibilities to territorial control. Through the early 1980s, there were numerous demands for limits on the power of the commissioner, including a defeated 1983 motion to remove the commissioner entirely from the legislature and turn his office into the equivalent of a provincial lieutenant governor. In response to this pressure, John Munro, minister of Indian affairs and northern development, announced that the commissioner's role would continue until land claims had been settled and the territorial political climate had stabilized. There was more movement at the administrative level. Control of the Departments of Information and Public Service were transferred from the commissioner's office to the Executive Council in 1983 and in April 1988 the NWT government announced that it had assumed full control over health services.

A central thrust of this political restructuring was a demand for a substantial realignment of territorial boundaries and political structures. The NWT administration created a Special Committee on Unity in November 1979 to investigate means of enhancing political consensus within the NWT. A lengthy series of discussions and consultations followed between the five-member committee and individuals, communities, and such Native organizations as the Inuit Tapirisat, Dene Nation, the Metis Association and COPE. The final report observed:

> The Northwest Territories as a geo-political jurisdiction simply does not inspire a natural sense of identity amongst many of its indigenous peoples; its government does not enjoy in the most fundamental sense the uncompromising loyalty and commitment of significant numbers of those who are now subject to it...it came into being essentially without the consent of those who inhabited the area.
>
> The federal government did not ask the inhabitants: Shall we keep these residual lands as one territory under a single government? It did not seek such consent, one can assume, because it felt that the inhabitants of the area were too few and, being largely unsophisticated in a political sense, were not then ready to make any judgement concerning this matter.

Moreover, it undoubtedly viewed the arrangement then as an interim agreement, to be altered when some other part(s) of the Territory seemed ready for provincial status.

In making this bold demand for the political change, the government was simply reacting to the erratic and illogical evolution of the NWT's boundaries. From 1870, the NWT had been Canada's leftovers, those lands and peoples that had not yet been fully integrated into the national economy and society. Over time, segments were carved off what had once been a huge land mass. The process, started with the creation of the province of Manitoba, continued through the establishment of the Yukon Territory, the creation of Alberta and Saskatchewan, and later deletions as a result of the northward extension of the provinces of Manitoba, Ontario and Quebec. The remaining land continued within a single political jurisdiction — the Northwest Territories.

The NWT, however, was a vast and culturally varied region. Settlements were isolated and widely dispersed. In addition, the very different paths of the two regions — the Mackenzie River Valley and the Eastern Arctic — only increased the sense of difference. Inuit dominated the Eastern Arctic, making up a sizeable majority of the regional population. The western district was more diverse, with a substantial Inuit population in the Mackenzie Delta, large numbers of Dene and Metis in the Mackenzie Valley and an important, if largely transient, non-Native population as well. So long as the NWT government was centered in Ottawa, the differing social and economic realities of the eastern and western Arctic were of little consequence. But as power devolved to the NWT government, the conflicting aspirations and needs of the communities and territorial regions took on greater importance.

Through the 1970s, debate over territorial autonomy and the continued transfer of federal responsibilities to regional control took on a new dimension. Led by political representatives from the Eastern Arctic, residents began to demand the division of the Northwest Territories. Some protested the whole concept, and argued for maintaining the integrity of the Territories. Many more, while accepting the concept in principle, disagreed on the boundary for the proposed new territories.

After giving agreement in principle to division and recommending a territorial plebiscite on the matter, the legislative assembly created a Special Committee on Constitutional Development in May 1981 to consider possible models for governments in newly created Territories. On April 14, 1982, voters who met the three-year eligibility requirement went to the polls to pass judgement on the proposed division. Fifty-three percent voted; of those, fifty-six percent favoured division. For territorial and federal decision-makers, the seemingly clear message was clouded by the fact that support was uneven across the Territory; the Eastern Arctic offered a strong mandate, but the western regions were considerably less supportive. Aboriginal organizations and the NWT government created a NWT Constitutional Alliance, later divided into the Western Constitutional Forum, and the Nunavut (Eastern Arctic) Constitutional Forum was soon in place as well. Negotiations then began with the federal government.

Matters would not proceed as smoothly as first anticipated. An extensive study by geographer William Wonders of the University of Alberta provided the cultural and economic data necessary to settle the demarcation line across the mainland. But a major problem developed with Inuit communities of the Western Arctic. Although these communities were culturally and linguistically aligned with the Inuit of Nunavut, they were closely tied to the politics and economics of the west. Equally, the COPE settlement district contained the much-coveted oil rich areas of the Mackenzie Delta and Beaufort Sea. The Western Arctic was reluctant to surrender this area, unless there was to be some form of revenue-sharing arrangement covering the region's resources. For these and other reasons, negotiations stalled, and acrimony replaced the post-plebiscite euphoria. Although division still claims hundreds of enthusiastic supporters across the Northwest Territories, it has been relegated to the political back-burner. The regional struggles inherent in the size and structure of the Northwest Territories ensures, however, that the issue is unlikely to disappear.

In the absence of a restructuring of territorial boundaries, the Northwest Territories government has proceeded with a devolution process of its own. The distance between most NWT communities and the different cultural and ethnic character of those settlements, has long worked against centralized administration. While the government is not actively promoting the regionalization of its administrative functions and does not view this process as an alternative to division, NWT officials have responded to requests from communities for greater local control. Rather than following a specific model for regional government, devolution has proceeded on a case-by-case process, transferring authority to community or regional bodies as is deemed appropriate and as is requested by the citizens involved.

Although there have been problems with the administrative restructuring of the Northwest Territories, particularly the daunting work-load placed on community leaders, the process has been accompanied by much excitement. The throwing off of the most direct and restrictive shackles of colonialism — demonstrated through the establishment of local health committees, Native participation on wildlife management boards and a variety of other administrative and political activities — has given the NWT a degree of autonomy and self-confidence that seemed unattainable fifteen or twenty years ago.

The Meech Lake Betrayal

Ironically, in the midst of major improvements in territorial authority, the Yukon and Northwest Territories received a cruel political blow. Just as the northern colonies moved towards equality, the constitutional process of the 1980s re-asserted federal dominance over the Territories, making them "forever colonies." Although there was increasing evidence through the late 1970s and early 1980s that national politicians were prepared to take northern issues seriously, there were few constitutional assurances of continued involvement. Increased consultation, which drew northern officials closer to the inner circle, served to heighten regional demands for constitutional equity. Its expectations rising rapidly, the North was to be bitterly disappointed.

When the Trudeau administration proceeded with its plans to patriate the British North America Act, the NWT and Yukon governments found that many of their aspirations had been ignored. There was particular concern in the northern assemblies about Ottawa's willingness to abandon aboriginal rights in the new constitution. But there were other issues, too. Provincial premiers, concerned that the federal government might abuse its power to create new provinces in order to erode provincial authority, advocated consultation before any new partners were added to Confederation. The provinces seemed to win, for the Constitution bill introduced in 1981 called for the involvement of the existing provinces in the creation of new provinces, a sharp break with tradition. That November, the entire NWT Legislative Assembly travelled to Ottawa to protest the federal proposals, joining hundreds of other voices of concern. While an imprecise statement on aboriginal rights made it into the final draft, a resolution of the question of process for the creation of future provinces would await a new government and a new constitutional process.

When Prime Minister Mulroney and the ten provincial premiers gathered at Meech Lake to seek amendments to the Constitution Act of 1982, the Territories were not invited. This slight hurt for, as Yukon Government Leader Tony Penikett observed, "our fates were as much or more at stake as Quebec's or any other province's." Further, he argued, it was "not necessary to sacrifice the North in order to save Quebec." Before Meech Lake, the federal government had the authority to create new provinces; under the agreement, the approval of all ten provinces would now be required. With no consultation, the Yukon and Northwest Territories discovered that their hope of eventually becoming equal partners in confederation had been all but tossed aside. The Territories were also denied the opportunity to participate in the recommendation of candidates for the senate and the supreme court. Such was the nature of Canadian constitution-making that the federal government and provincial premiers were prepared to sacrifice the aspirations of a disadvantaged region in order to achieve other political objectives.

The northern Territories did not accept the Meech Lake betrayal quietly. Tony Penikett was particularly outspoken in his opposition to the accord, leading a territorial court challenge and demanding a reconsideration of the agreement. Following a Yukon Territorial Court decision awarding a trial on the case, the British Columbia Court of Appeal accepted the federal government position that the Meech Lake accord did not violate Yukoners' rights under the Charter of Rights. The Northwest Territories government was not silent on the issue. Government Leaders Norm Sibbeston and Donald Patterson joined Penikett and other northern politicians in actively campaigning on the matter. The NWT joined with the Yukon in an unsuccessful 1988 Supreme Court of Canada challenge.

The Meech Lake controversy is filled with irony. It represents an assault on Northerners' constitutional rights — an example of Canadian brokerage politics ignoring the rights of a minority. In their haste to placate Quebec, a laudable and important goal, the first ministers uncaringly trampled on the political aspirations of its constitutionally weakest members. The requirement for unanimous approval — unlikely, given the provinces' tendency to protect their powers and various regional interests in extending provincial status northward — effectively limits the dream of northern constitutional reforms. At the same time, debate over constitutional reform has united Northerners like few issues have in the past. In the Yukon federal by-election of 1987, all three candidates protested the accord, breaking with their national parties in the process. The Yukon and Northwest Territories have identified a common cause and have coordinated protest efforts, a surprisingly rare occurance in the last two decades. Matters and slights like these are likely to generate a sustained regional protest and form the basis for a strong regional identity.

The timing of the constitutional controversy is perhaps the greatest irony, for it comes in the midst of the modernization of northern politics and administration. After fifteen years of devolution, increased autonomy and political experimentation and maturation, the Yukon and Northwest Territories had every reason to believe that even better times lay ahead. Meech Lake hammered home, as few government or political actions could, that not all that much had really changed.

The controversy over Meech Lake has diverted attention away from the substantial political gains made in the North over the past two decades. The introduction of political parties in the Yukon, the creation of consensus government in the Northwest Territories and the continuing process of devolution have reshaped the way the North administers its affairs and plans for its future. Canada's colonies are still colonies, but they have developed substantially from the truncated and immature political cultures that were in place twenty years ago.

The modern Whitehorse subdivision of Riverdale could fit easily in most southern cities — except for the profusion of wood-burning stoves.

Parks Canada has devoted millions of dollars to the refurbishing of Dawson City, keeping alive the mystique of the Klondike Gold Rush.

The company town of Faro was all but abandoned in the early 1980s, when the mine closed down. The town, and the mine, have since reopened.

The Alaska Highway, substantially repaved and reconstructed, is a major access route to the northwest. Most of the tourists simply pass through the Yukon
on their way to Alaska.

Whitehorse, capital city of the Yukon, is home to well over half of the territory's population and is a major government centre.

The Porcupine River caribou herd, some 100,000 strong, migrates between the northern Yukon and northern Alaska each year. The U.S. government is currently considering a request to open the caribou breeding grounds for oil exploration.

The Tatshenshini River, long an important source of food for Native people, is now popular among fishermen and white water rafters.

The South Klondike Highway, connecting Carcross and Skagway, was initially designed for summer tourist traffic. It is now open year-round.

Traditional activities, such as preparing seal skins, form an important part of the northern economy. Maggie Akrajuk of Pangnirtung is stretching a seal skin.

Many Native people continue to spend large parts of the year on the land. Lilliam Shamee, shown here with her sons, is from Eskimo Point.

Native people have made major strides in regaining control of their affairs. Gatherings such as this meeting of the Dogrib Tribal Council at Snare Lake form a vital part of the NWT's political structure.

Downtown Yellowknife, capital city of the Northwest Territories.

The NWT legislative assembly operates in an unusual (for most Canadians) consensus fashion. There are no formal political parties.

A modern version of the northern "treaty time," when the Natives received their annuities from the government and discussed business with government agents. Colville Lake, 1978.

Native home, Fort Rae, NWT.

Thomas Berger, Mackenzie Valley Pipeline Inquiry, Yellowknife, 1977.

Cape Dorset, NWT, 1975.

Dog sleds were long the primary means of winter transportation in the north. By the late 1960s many hunters had given up their dog teams for skidoos, but more recently there has been a move back to the dog teams.

4

Northern Service: Bureaucrats and the Territories

Civil servants form a vital component of northern society, providing a much-needed measure of economic and social stability, as well as generating and administering the programs that make the region one of the most administratively innovative in the country. They dominate the North's largest centres — Whitehorse and Yellowknife — and provide an educated, professional group that has brought the North much of its spirit and vitality. Because they exert such influence over the expenditure of government funds, the bureaucrats are also a potent political force in the North.

This same power and presence, not surprisingly, carries considerable risks. The free enterprise ethos that permeates the northern business community, particularly the mining sector, often collides with the pace and administrative overburden of the civil service. Similarly, the vestiges of colonial rule have not been completely removed, and remain evident in aspects of the relationship between bureaucrats and Native people. Such qualifications aside — and there are some important and telling criticisms of the civil service in the North — the expansion, empowerment and regionalization of the federal and territorial bureaucracies are essential elements in the development of the modern North.

The Bureaucratic Presence

Until World War II, the federal government assigned only a small contingent of public servants to northern responsibilities, and many of those worked in Ottawa. From 1939 to 1949, the governance of the territories fell to the Department of Mines and Resources, restructured in 1949 as the Department of Resources and Development. In 1953, the federal government announced the creation of the Department of Northern Affairs and National Resources, a symbol of a growing commitment to the land north of the sixtieth parallel. That structure remained in place until 1966, when the Department of Indian Affairs and Northern Development was created.

Within this departmental structure, operations in the North were administered by specific agencies: the Northwest Territories and Yukon Branch between 1922 and 1951, Northern Administration and Lands Branch from 1951 to 1971 and the Northern Affairs Program from 1971 to the present. This last change improved the profile and coordination of northern matters within the federal civil service. The Northern Affairs Program supported territorial and municipal governments and assisted with welfare, education and health. At the same time, it encouraged the development of northern resources, supporting the construction of roads, airports, communications systems, oil, gas and mineral exploration and environmental management.

Not all federal affairs in the North could be contained under one roof. The Indian and Inuit Affairs Branch had specific responsibility for Native matters, covering everything from local government, social assistance and housing to band membership, economic development and education. This branch also handled treaty negotiations, enfranchisement and reserve allocations. The IIAB and the NAP have often been at odds, since they represent the frequently conflicting aspirations of Native and non-Native Northerners. The oddity of compressing them into a single government department, under a single minister, has been repeatedly commented on, but nevertheless remains unchanged.

The minister of the Department of Indian Affairs and Northern Development, responsible for a huge Ottawa-based establishment and its many northern arms, is the most powerful individual involved with the North. The power of the cabinet minister easily outstrips that of the members of parliament, government leaders in the Territories and territorial counsellors. The minister of IAND is a veritable czar ruling over close to half of Canada's land mass. Despite the comparatively slight attention granted to the northern Territories by the federal government, the cabinet post has long been a favourite. Former ministers (since 1970) Jean Chrètien, Judd Buchanan, Warren Allmand, Hugh Faulkner, Jake Epp, John Munro, David Crombie and Bill McKnight have all spoken enthusiastically about their time in office, typically describing their work with Native people and the North as the highlight of their career. (It is too soon to tell if the same is true of the current minister, Pierre Cadieux.) The attraction is fairly obvious — exotic locations, vast distances, a varied workload and an opportunity to assist with the revitalization of northern Native cultures and the rapid transition of northern life generally.

The minister of IAND is not the only cabinet minister with northern responsibilities. In fact, in 1984/1985, less than twenty percent of all federal civil servants with northern responsibilities actually worked for this department. Other departments with sizeable northern contingents included Defence (seventeen percent of all federal employees), Health and Welfare (sixteen percent), Environment (ten percent), Transport (nine percent) and the Royal Canadian Mounted Police (less than nine percent). In total, the federal civil service complement is quite substantial. In 1973/74, some 4,485 person years were assigned to northern service; by 1983/1984, the number had grown to over 4,900. The first years of Conservative rule have seen a significant roll-back; the government planned for slightly over 4,700 person years, not including crown corporations.

Northerners, pleased with the apparent simplicity of life in the region, have long been baffled by the complexity of the federal administrative apparatus. Consider the Department of Indian and Northern Affairs in 1981/1982. The Northern Program was responsible for northern resources, the environment, Native cultures and languages and the political evolution of the territories. There were a number of branches within the program. The Policy and Programming Branch was to coordinate federal and territorial activities; the Northern Policy Directorate would oversee policy, planning, Native claims and co-ordination; the Northern Co-ordination and Social Development Directorate, to confuse matters, had divisions of territorial relations, research and a social and cultural development division, which in turn had five sections: Native liaison, Inuit art, culture and linguistics, vocational training and loan fund and administration.

There is more. The Northern Program also had under it the following: Major Projects Assessment Directorate, Northern Environment division (including land management, land use planning, forest resources and water); Northern Environmental Protection Branch, Northern Resources and Economic Planning, Northern Economic Planning Directorate (with divisions of Forecast and Analysis, Transportation and Communications, Native Economy and Renewable Resources Development, non-Renewable Resources Development, and Energy Planning); Northern Roads and Airstrips Directorate; and Socio-Economic Agreements Directorate. One of the largest divisions in IAND is the Indian and Inuit Affairs Program, which has subdivisions of Resource Developments Impact, Economic and Employment Development, Social Development, Education, Local Government and Reserves and Trusts.

The lines of responsibility within IAND are not as precise as this list suggests, since there is considerable overlap with other government agencies. The Canadian Transport Commission and the departments of Communications, Employment and Immigration, Energy, Mines and Resources, and Environment have legislative responsibilities in the North that are close to the activities of the DIAND. Much of this has been handled through close inter-departmental liaison, but the overlap only clouds an already unclear situation. The proliferation of government programs, exacerbated by the steady growth of independent territorial administrations, complicates the work of bureaucrats and those seeking to approach government.

Take, for example, the matter of resource development. According to one report, "at least nine federal departments and agencies, as well as the two territorial governments, are directly involved in the administration of northern resource and environmental legislation and regulations. Not included in this number are special purpose interdepartmental and intragovernmental coordinating committees, task forces, special agencies, parliamentary committees and native land-claims negotiating teams, whose decisions influence northern environmental and resource management." The federal government is involved in northern resource development through the departments of Indian Affairs and Northern Development, Environment, Fisheries and Oceans, Health and Welfare, Energy, Mines and Resources and Transport, as well as the National Energy Board, the Atomic Energy Control Board and the Canada Oil and Gas Lands Administration.

There is a similar overlap in the area of economic development initiatives in the North. Several years ago, the Yukon territorial government created the "One Stop Shop," a central agency to administer all economic and business programs offering assistance for individuals and businesses. The centre provided help with twenty-five different federal and territorial programs; surprisingly, however, the government acknowledged that there were actually over ninety separate economic development programs. No wonder, then, that individuals, businessmen, Native groups and others approaching officialdom have often complained about the jungle of government programs, agencies and offices in existence in the North.

The overlap and proliferation of government services in the Canadian North has become a cause for considerable concern. With the departments and agencies headquartered in Ottawa, with regional offices for federal departments in southern centres, and with duties obscured by a tangled web of federal and territorial responsibilities, government has become increasingly complex. This may, however, be something of a transitory phase between the federal neglect of the pre-1950 era and the steady advance of territorial autonomy. As the Yukon and Northwest Territories gain increasing self-government, the duplication and overlap should recede.

The steady progress of devolution and the expanding activities of the NWT and Yukon governments are readily apparent through employment figures. In 1973/74, the NWT allocated just over 2,800 person years for its departments. By 1984/85, that number had risen to almost 3,400. Estimates for 1986/87 called for over 3,800 person years of employment. The growth in the Yukon has similarly been rapid. There were 1,238 people employed in the Yukon territorial administration in 1973; in 1986, there were over 2,350 territorial workers (and an additional 237 municipal employees).

When the territorial and federal numbers are combined, the figures are staggering. Forecasts for 1985/1986 called for 10,100 civil service person years of employment for the Canadian North, a region inhabited by approximately 70,000 people in total. Not all these bureaucrats, of course, live in the Territories. In 1985, slightly fewer than 1,300 federal employees worked in the Yukon Territory; almost 2,650 lived in the Northwest Territories. While this is a sizeable majority of the close to 4,800 person years of federal employment assigned to northern service, it still leaves a sizeable component outside the North. Nevertheless, the northern civil service represents a very prominent demographic force in the region.

Government payrolls, logically, contribute a sizeable boost to the territorial economies. In 1978, federal expenditures on employees in the Yukon totalled almost $20 million; by 1985, the payroll had expanded to $35.4 million. There was a similar expansion in the neighbouring Northwest Territories, where the federal government payroll grew from $46 million in 1980 to over $64 million in 1986. In the Northwest Territories, the territorial payroll jumped from over $76 million in 1980 to over $182.8 million six years later. Over the same period, Yukon government expenditures on the territorial payroll increased from $33 million to $78.8 million. The total government payroll in the Yukon (federal, territorial and municipal) exceeded $120 million in 1985; in the NWT, the sum was just short of $270 million. An additional

1,200 employees of federal crown corporations also work in the North.

While the employment and payroll figures provide further evidence of the importance of the northern civil service, they tell only part of the story. Equally significant is the fact that federal and territorial bureaucrats control large amounts of the taxpayers' money. Again, the numbers give an indication of the scale, and the growth, of government expenditures over the past fifteen years. In 1973/74, federal and territorial governments spent over $353 million in the North, with the lion's share, almost $200 million, coming directly from the federal government. The Yukon government spent almost $41 million; the Northwest Territories government handled over $115 million. By 1984, total government expenditures had risen to $1,450,000,000. Approximately half — $721 million — came from the federal government, with the NWT spending almost $570 million and the Yukon $166 million. However, the division of monies is a bit misleading. Over fifty-five percent of the Yukon's budget comes through federal transfer payments; in the Northwest Territories, the number is around sixty-eight percent.

Federal money is delivered to the North in a variety of ways, including direct grants, departmental and agencies expenditures, and subsidy programs for individuals or businesses. One of the more prominent of these programs, targeted at aboriginal people, is the special ARDA (Agricultural and Rural Development) initiative, created in 1970 by the Department of Regional Economic Expansion. Between 1978 and 1986, over 150 Yukon applications, worth over $6 million, were approved. The funding provided assistance for training and staff for the Council of Yukon Indians, trapping, Native crafts, gas stations, recreational vehicle parks, trail rides and outfitters, construction companies and other small enterprises. Results have been uneven, due partly to the structural barriers to Native business and partly to a complex application process (the federal government provides counsellors to assist with applications.). There is a similar situation in the Northwest Territories, where the mix of government initiatives includes a NWT Co-operative Business Development fund, regional tourism development strategies, a new Venture

Capital Program, and a Tourism Training and Manpower Needs Board.

There are, however, many other economic development programs, some available to all Canadians, other designed specifically for the North. The acronyms are more than a bit confusing, the proliferation of programs bewildering. Over the past decade, there have been LEAP and LEAD, NEED, Job Corps, Canada Works, Canada Access, Summer Canada Program, Northern Careers Program, Indian Community Human Resources Strategies Program and others. There is, of course, a political explanation for this program growth. The short-term requirements of the democratic process place a real priority on regular announcements of new government initiatives, targeted at specific economic needs. The needs of the political masters have ensured that northern commercial development schemes have been overwhelmed by a complex proliferation of programs, bureaucratic overlap, and confusion among potential applicants.

Lately there has been a major and substantial shift in the structure of federal-territorial assistance programs. The Canada-Yukon Economic Development Agreement, signed first in 1985 and recently renewed, seeks to provide stability in government initiatives and to broaden the region's economic base. The EDA is further divided into a series of sub-agreements — on renewable resources, tourism, Economic Development Planning, Yukon Business Loans and a special grant for restarting the Faro mine. The Northwest Territories has a similar EDA, prepared in consultation with over 100 NWT organizations and covering six subsidiary agreements: small business, arts and crafts, mining, tourism, renewable resources and regional economic strategies. The EDAs are designed to provide greater territorial and Native control over to the disbursement of government grants and the determination of economic policy for the region.

The federal government, obviously, contributes massively to the financial support of the northern Territories. According to Gordon Robertson, "The two Territories received, per capita, 5.6 times as much in federal transfers as the province with the largest equalization transfers." He continued:

Differences of this kind do not reflect wanton ex-
travagance by the territorial administration. They are
the financial reflection of what everyone familiar with
the North knows; costs of virtually everything are
much higher than in the South. Distances are enormous, population is sparse, the country is at an early
stage of development with great need for economic
and social infrastructure, the climate is cruel, building
conditions are difficult, and commodities from
'outside' must come long distances at high cost.

Tracing these expenditures through the myriad departments and
programs is a complex undertaking. The dispersal of the civil
servants — some northern departments report directly to Ottawa
while others are part of regional offices — further clouds any
understanding of the situation. The Department of Public Works,
for example, was responsible for the Alaska Highway from 1964
to 1972, when it transferred maintenance responsibility for the
Yukon sections to the territorial government. That department,
however, worked through the Pacific Region, and has long been
supervised out of Vancouver. Many of the NWT divisions of
federal departments report through Alberta departmental offices. In the case of Parks Canada, which itself has been shuffled
between federal ministries, its responsibilities in the Yukon and
Northwest Territories are administered out of a Winnipeg office.

The Changing Face of Territorial Bureaucracy

The federal bureaucracy has had considerable problems with its
northern responsibilities. The transiency of its employees, the
distance between Ottawa and the field offices, and the cultural
barriers between its largely southern-raised staff and its northern
constituents have interfered with the implementation of government programs. Whatever its failings, however, the federal
bureaucracy can at least call on a rich tradition of public service.
    The same does not necessarily hold for the territorial govern-
ments. For many years the only civil servants in the North, except
for the police and a small cadre of surveyors and scientists,

worked for the Department of Indian Affairs and Northern Development. As the territorial autonomy and responsibilities expanded, the governments of the Yukon and Northwest Territories scrambled to keep up with the growth. The results have been uneven.

The civil service in the Northwest Territories is still in transition. Until the Carrothers Commission, and the transfer of the capital to Yellowknife, the Territories' bureaucratic presence in the North was weak. While the civil service has grown rapidly since that time, the politically astute process of regionalization has produced a certain degree of fragmentation in the territorial bureaucracy. The government of the Northwest Territories has been divided into eleven departments, each operating within the five regions in the territory. There is a regional superintendent for each department; the superintendents have considerable autonomy in their day-to-day activities and have even started to develop independent policies suitable for their region.

Although there are administrative problems with such a decentralized system — a further indication of why territorial division has so many supporters — it does respond to the social and political realities of the north. In the 1950s, the federal government dispatched a number of Northern Service Officers to train Native people for administrative and political service. The officers actually assumed much of the power themselves, imposing a southern-style administrative structure on the region. The Carrothers Commission enhanced the process, encouraging the integration of local-level government into the Northwest Territories' administration. In 1978, over half the communities were still of settlement status; local councils had only an advisory function, with little control over the issues that really mattered — education, social programs and land-use provisions. Over the past decade, however, much has been done to empower local governments. The territorial assembly has provided local communities with a greater measure of self-government on a range of matters. This exercise, which has expanded rapidly in the fields of education, health and resource management, seeks to give Native communities real control over their lives while offering a northern, not a southern, model for territorial administration.

The territorial government, following the lead of the federal government, is also committed to increasing the number of Native people and their decision-making authority within the civil service. Non-Native people not only tend to stay in the North for a short time, they also inevitably carry with them the cultural baggage of their southern origins. The move toward involving aboriginal people in the civil service, therefore, is a deliberate attempt to address one of the North's longstanding and most pressing problems. The "indigenization" of the government workforce, built around a "hire Native" policy introduced by the government in the early 1970s, is just beginning to show promise but there is still a long way to go. Few northern Natives have been recruited into either the federal or territorial civil service. The reasons for this are many. There are more ideologically attractive opportunities with Native organizations. Further, there are actually few trained people available for the posts, since northern Inuit, Metis and Dene have relatively low levels of educational attainment. Perhaps most important, success in the civil service invariably requires relocation away from the home community, an unpalatable decision for many.

The territorial government's commitment to regionalization and Native hiring has other, potentially insidious, costs. Michael Wittington describes the situation:

> Generally, in the NWT a career in the public service requires significant experience in the field in the more remote communities before promotion to more senior positions in Yellowknife. One result of this career pattern has been that the senior management positions in the government have tended to be dominated by personnel lacking professional management training. The reason for this is that people with such training are generally unwilling to accept the relatively junior and generalist positions in the field, which are simply not challenging enough.... Even today there are disproportionate numbers of ex-teachers who have been

promoted to senior management because of higher
levels of formal education, and significant numbers of
ex-RCMP NCOs and ex-Bay employees who have had
the opportunity to acquire some supervisory skills in
their jobs.

This is changing, particularly in Yellowknife, where a large number of southern-trained professionals, many with little or no field
experience, are beginning to work their way through the civil
service. While such hirings have imported the professional ex-
pertise necessary to cope with the NWT's growing responsibilities, some difficulties have emerged. Tensions have grown
between the old-guard, who clearly preferred the small-scale,
decentralized pattern of the past, and the "upstarts." The technologically innovative new-guard has clearly modernized territorial administration, but the jury is still out on whether or not
this fast-paced modernization was actually necessary, given the
small population.

The situation in the Yukon is considerably different. A longer
history of government administration, stretching back to the
Klondike gold rush, and a larger and more concentrated non-Native population have provided the Yukon a more stable and
professional civil service. The Yukon is also aided by the fact that
its bureaucracy is much smaller, and centralized in Whitehorse.
The capital city's attractiveness to potential employees, combined with the Yukon government's lesser emphasis on the need
for field experience in the North and the existence of the Public
Service Commission, has resulted in the establishment of a bet-
ter-trained bureaucracy.

There are other differences between the Yukon and NWT
bureaucracies. Because of the smaller size of the Yukon's Native
population, the government of that Territory has not, until
recently, pursued the integration of Native people into the civil
service with the eagerness and commitment of the NWT. As well,
unlike its counterpart in the NWT, the Yukon's civil service is
highly centralized. That centralization reflects the smaller size of
the territory, easier communications and travel and the potential
for conflict within the ethnically mixed communities. Local Im-

provement Districts were established in the 1970s, offering a narrow range of powers (garbage, roads, sewers) to smaller communities, but they remained primarily advisory. In 1980, the Yukon Government eliminated the Local Improvement District; smaller communities were allowed to become hamlets or unincorporated settlements. The situation is much like that which existed in the Northwest Territories in the 1970s, and is unlikely to change in the near future.

The process of devolution, discussed earlier at a policy level, also had an important administrative side. By passing on some of its responsibilities to the territorial governments, Ottawa also made it possible for federal civil servants to follow their jobs to the Yukon and NWT. For example, when responsibility for the Alaska Highway was transferred to the Yukon government in 1972, highway workers were afforded the opportunity to join the territorial bureaucracy. Some stayed with the federal government, some left government service altogether, but the majority moved to the Yukon Department of Highways. The process continues. The devolution of forestry responsibilities to the NWT government in the mid-1980s, for example, resulted in the transfer of 122 employees.

Bureaucracy and Health Care: A Case Study

Recent changes in the health care field illustrate both the pace of recent changes, and the need for continued progress in the decolonization of the North. Providing adequate health care for the widely scattered regional population has long perplexed federal government administrators. After World War II, the government built new nursing stations, removed people with tuberculosis to southern treatment centres and greatly expanded its expenditures on health care. The effort was much needed, especially for the aboriginal people, who were suffering from the ill effects of imported diseases and food shortages.

The rapid growth caused many problems. Health care professionals carried a southern and western medical ideology into the North. Their authoritarian interventionist manner matched the expectations of most Canadians, but stood in stark contrast to

Native traditions. Further, many of the new medical practices introduced by the southern doctors and nurses revealed a lack of concern for the cultural needs of their Native patients. Medical anthropologist John O'Neill described the impact:

> The message implicit in this treatment approach was that responsibility for decisions regarding the type and location of treatment for diseases was now entirely in the hands of the colonial power. Furthermore, medicine had the authority to disrupt family life and traditional patterns of social organization…. Instead of sickness being viewed as an event which, with the help of a healer, resulted in increased social harmony and integration, illness now facilitated intrusion of the colonial power into the intimacies of family life.

The birthing process in the Northwest Territories provides one of the best examples. By the 1970s, the government had decreed, for medical reasons, that babies would be born in properly equipped hospitals. Since there were only nursing stations in most small, isolated communities, this meant that expectant mothers had to be flown to a larger centre — usually Yellowknife, Iqaluit or Churchill, Manitoba — to await the birth of their children. While this suited the medical requirements, ensuring mother and child of proper professional care, the process eliminated family and community involvement with the birth. Mothers were often separated from their husbands and families for several weeks, longer if there were troubles with the pregnancy or birth. The government and medical professionals argued that this was required to protect mother and child; if a serious problem occurred during a home birth, the mother or child or both might well die. Many Native women, however, wanted the right to decide for themselves if their children would be born at home or in a distant community.

The medical profession, particularly nursing, has changed with the times, but this has created new problems. Over the past decade, greater emphasis has been placed on self-help — changes to nutrition and lifestyle rather than on immediate recourse to medicine — a sharp break from earlier interventionist standards. Northern Natives, however, have not always responded favourably to the new system. Born and raised under the old colonial model of health care, Native people have often demanded more interventionist measures than the professionals are prepared to provide, insisting, for example, that prescription medicines be provided when the doctor wishes a change in eating habits.

There were other problems. Native people were seldom treated in their own language, for few health care professionals were conversant in northern tongues. Hospital food, prepared with due care to national nutritional standards, was often unacceptable to Native patients, particularly the elderly, who had been raised on country food. These factors only added to the unattractiveness of a hospital visit and heightened distrust of the medical fraternity. Little wonder, then, that Native people have led the fight for regional control of medical care.

The situation has take a dramatic turn in the past few years. Native organizations, particularly women's groups, have demanded greater control over the health care system. The federal government, committed to the devolution process, has turned over control of medical care to the territorial governments. The NWT administration, in turn, has indicated a determination to give community-level bodies significant input into planning and management. In one observer's words, the process has "turned the cumbersome, overlapping jurisdictions of the administration of health care into a responsive, locally directed system, almost overnight." As of April 1, 1988, a community health committee in each settlement assumed control of local health care delivery. In addition, each community has representation on one of the nine regional health boards.

While many applaud the move to "self-determination" in this critical field, a number of health-care practitioners are worried about the growing influence of non-professionals in their field. A number of doctors and nurses, raised and trained in southern, urban settings, will undoubtedly be troubled by the transfer of responsibilities to Native-run committees and boards. Given the legacy of colonialism in northern health care, however, a dramatic step is clearly necessary. As John O'Neill argues: "Self-determination in Native health care is a public health movement of historic proportions and the effective delivery of the full range of preventive, curative and educational health services in the North will not progress until the transfer is complete."

The transformation of Northern health care is more than just ideological. There has been a tremendous expansion in facilities over the past two decades. In 1983, for example, the Medical Services Branch operated in the Yukon a general hospital, three cottage hospitals, two nursing stations, ten health centres and four health stations. In the Northwest Territories, there were four hospitals, two cottage hospitals, thirty-nine nursing stations, eight health centres and several health stations. The construction and technical boom has proceeded apace; among the new facilities is a 135-bed hospital for Yellowknife, which opened in the spring of 1988. The use of satellite transmissions to link nursing stations and southern hospitals has further addressed the traditional isolation of northern health care professionals. Satellite connections permit the transmission of x-ray data over thousands of miles, aiding in diagnosis and treatment for patients in isolated communities.

This new communications technology helps offset the North's chronic shortage of doctors. In 1982, the Yukon had more general practitioners than the national average; the NWT's rate, conversely, was half that of Canada as a whole. While there is usually little difficulty attracting medical staff to Whitehorse, the same is not true for outlying districts. In 1988, the town of Faro ran a high-profile national campaign in a successful attempt to recruit a permanent physician, offering a generous compensation and support package in return for a promise to relocate to the mining community. The real problem, however, is with specialists. There were almost 5,800 Yukoners per specialist physician in 1982; in the NWT the rate was over 4,000 residents per specialist. The national average was slightly over 1,250.

The North has found ways of combatting what is a fairly inevitable problem. Stanton Yellowknife Hospital, for example, operates a central specialistic program, but has also begun to take these services on the road. Outside specialists are also brought into the region on periodic visitations. In emergency cases, residents are quickly flown out of their own community — to Whitehorse, Yellowknife or Iqaluit, or to southern centres if the problem is deemed serious enough. This movement "outside," of course, carries its own problems, since the patient and family must readjust to southern settings.

Measures are being taken to address this concern. The Baffin Regional Health Board, established in 1986, recently opened a receiving home in Montreal for patients sent outside for care. Baffin House, as it is called, has an Inuit staff, keeps in contact with the patient's family and generally expedites and smooths the invariably rough transition. It is a small initiative, but an important one in that it recognizes the problems inherent in being removed from an isolated northern community and sent to a technologically advanced hospital in a southern city.

Health care was one of the first government services extended into the Canadian North; it is now among the first to be brought under northern and Native control. Affirmative action programs and specialized training courses at Yukon College and Arctic College are drawing more Inuit, Dene and Metis into the medical professions. Native employment in these fields in the Baffin district, for instance, jumped from fourteen percent in 1982 to thirty-seven percent six years later. The process remains far from complete. The national medical profession, perennially suspicious of curative measures from other traditions, has made only the most tentative steps towards incorporating Native healing into health care. Native women are particularly concerned about their treatment by the medical profession. And non-Native people, often used to the ready availability of a full range of medical services, remain troubled by the less than complete coverage of the northern Territories.

The Revolution in Northern Bureaucracy

Civil servants are a large and potent force in the Canadian North. The post-1985 Yukon provides perhaps the best illustration of the power and opportunity that lies within the bureaucracy. Kept in check by the free-enterprise Conservative administration in the first years of responsible government (a process aided by a steadily deepening depression in the early 1980s), the bureaucracy came to life under the NDP government. The new administration's innovative planning initiative, the Yukon 2000 process, made it clear that the government was open to new ideas; the civil servants responded with a range of suggestions and programs. Since then, bureaucrats have played an important and innovative role in the Yukon's return to economic health.

The non-partisan tradition of NWT politics, and the smaller scale of the administration, have similarly given considerable latitude to civil servants in that jurisdiction. Striking new measures — from the physical expansion and program development of Yukon College to the NWT Department of Education's Native language programs — belies the standard image of intransigent and uncreative bureaucrats and gives an indication of the role of the civil service in the modernization of the North.

Devolution presents the North with its greatest administrative challenge. For the past two decades, having won much of the political battle for responsible government, the territorial governments have been demanding the transfer of administrative responsibilities. The federal government has gradually accepted that request, offering the power, money and personnel that northern politicians have long claimed is essential for regional self-determination. While some resistance persists in the middle ranks of the civil service, there is no doubt that federal politicians and senior administrators are committed to passing on real and substantial power to the Territories. There are some outstanding problems, such as continued administrative overlap, the proliferation of federal and territorial programs, and the need to reconcile Native and non-Native perspectives and needs, but there is also a great deal of promise in this change.

For the past century, the federal civil service has been the principal agency of colonial control and regulation. Federal agents from the Mounted Police, the Department of Indian Affairs, the Geological Survey, the Department of Mines and other agencies gathered the knowledge, implemented the programs and did Ottawa's bidding in the land north of sixty. Northerners resented the southern control; Native people struggled with the cultural insensitivity and domination of the national bureaucracy. That power has now been significantly reduced and the North finds itself in the midst of an administrative revolution. The early stages of the decolonization of the civil service have given the Yukon and the Northwest Territories the tools they need to fashion their own future.

5

Fighting for Control: Native Politics and Land Claims

In the halcyon days of the 1960s resource boom, scant attention was paid to the few questions, complaints and suggestions coming out of Native communities in the North. Non-Native administrators and politicians felt comfortable in ignoring aboriginal voices, for in their view the rapid expansion of the welfare state in the North provided ample evidence of Canadian concern for Native peoples. Those few Natives speaking out in defence of traditional lifestyles were dismissed as voices from the past.

The Native people came together slowly throughout the late 1960s. To be sure, there were lots of white advisors around. Community development workers sent by the Department of Indian Affairs and representatives of the Company of Young Canadians came north to organize aboriginal people to stand up for their rights. These people often had their own ideological or political axes to grind, and occasionally led Native people down paths they soon found unacceptable. In time, the power of the white advisors was reduced, replaced by a cadre of young, politicized, educated and often angry Native activists. For years, however, the early presence of white "agitators" would continue to colour the perception of aboriginal organizations held by non-Native Northerners and government officials. Long after the Native people had gained control over their organizations and established their own agenda for political, social and economic change, they continued to be accused of being mere front-men for white advisors. Few non-Natives wanted to see beyond what they perceived as a façade; only reluctantly, and after several years, would they recognize the deep commitment that lay behind the Native organizations and the land-claims battles across the north.

Native Organizations

The first problem for aboriginal people was learning to speak the political language of the colonizers. Hundreds of Native people had gone through residential schools across the North by the 1960s, but it would take the political and racial turmoil of that tumultuous decade to bring aboriginal protests into focus and provide direction for Native leaders who sought a better future for their people. In the 1960s, Native people across North America organized to protect their interests. While the media focused its attention on radical groups like the American Indian Movement (AIM), more moderate organizations attracted considerable interest in the Native communities.

The North presented a special challenge for Native organizers. The villages were widely scattered and, in the 1960s, most lacked even rudimentary communications with the outside world. Not well-informed of events around the Territories and across the country, and still pursuing a traditional economy, aboriginal people were reluctant to throw their support behind a protest movement. But the Native organizers kept to the task, much as union workers throughout Canada struggled with unreceptive audiences of workers earlier in the century. Slowly, individually, by family and eventually on a community-wide basis, the fieldworkers brought the Native constituents together. This little-known process of community organization, more important perhaps than the first approaches to government, laid the foundation for later protests and demands. The spread of the democratic process remained, however, a two-edged sword; Native leaders forgot at their peril that power in aboriginal organizations lay with the communities and not with the political leadership.

In the late 1960s, Native people were only too aware of government's lack of attention to their problems. The Department of Indian Affairs and Northern Development did meet once a year with a Chiefs' Advisory Council, but the Natives knew that their concerns went largely unnoticed. Department of Indian Affairs' workers, who shuffled in and out of the Territories on a regular basis, brought the values and attitudes of the south with them. There was little affinity for the Natives' harvesting activities or their culture. It was not that the government and its employees were unconcerned; an array of economic and social programs suggested that that is not so. Rather, the problem lay in the perpetuation of the long-standing non-Native and southern assumption that Native people could be aided only by speeding their integration into mainstream Canadian society. Although highly flawed, this assumption dominated government thinking for much of the post-war period.

Native people reacted against the colonial, paternalistic and racist assumptions that underlay much of the government's planning. In the Northwest Territories, the introduction of co-operatives in the late 1950s and 1960s provided an important training ground. Many of the Inuit leaders of the 1970s emerged out of the co-operative movement. Additional strength was found in the work of national Native organizations, like the National Indian Council, founded in 1961, and the National Indian Brotherhood and Canadian Metis Society, both founded in 1968. Other organizations helped out. In 1971, OXFAM gave a small plane to the Indian-Eskimo Association of Canada. Organizer Wally Firth, later member of parliament for the Northwest Territories, flew into communities across the North, working with Native organizations, helping to development programs and spreading word of the expansion of Native activism.

The organizational impulse was aided, ironically, by an ill-conceived federal initiative. In 1969, Jean Chrètien, Minister of Indian Affairs and Northern Development, introduced a White Paper on Indian Affairs in Canada. The proposal called for the elimination of the Department of Indian Affairs and the rapid integration of Native people into Canadian society. Native organizations across the country rose up in anger, denouncing the minister and the Trudeau government and demanding that the plan be scrapped. The protest was successful and the White Paper abandoned. More important, however, Native people had discovered the power of aboriginal organization.

Native organizations emerged on a regional basis, reflecting the cultural, linguistic, geographical and political barriers between aboriginal people across the North. The Yukon Native Brotherhood, led by Elijah Smith, was formed in 1968 and formally incorporated two years later. Non-status Indians organized separately; in October 1971, they formed the Yukon Association of Non-Status Indians (YANSI). The creation of YANSI rested on the legal discrimination inherent in the Indian Act, which permitted government statutes and regulations to determine an individual's status. In a cultural or ethnic sense, the status/non-status distinction had little cultural foundation in the Yukon Territory; there are no identifiable Metis settlements in the Yukon as there are in the neighbouring Northwest Territories. Both status and non-status Indians felt uncomfortable with the legally-mandated distinction between peoples who lived, worked and hunted together. The negotiation of a Yukon land claim hastened a merger. In 1973, the YNB and the YANSI joined to form the Council of Yukon Indians (CYI).

Since 1973, the Council of Yukon Indians has played a crucial role in Yukon life, its duties and responsibilities expanding considerably over the years. CYI, the official legislative body for Yukon Indians, allocates funds provided by the federal government, creates and supervises programs and coordinates land-claims negotiation. Not all Yukon Native people have been comfortable with the centralizing tendencies of the CYI. There are seven different language groups and thirteen bands in the Territory, ranging from those in isolated settlements like Old Crow, located north of the Arctic Circle and inaccessible by road, to the urban Kwanlin Dun (Whitehorse) band. Because of this diversity, the relationship between CYI and the communities has not always been smooth. In 1976, for example, the CYI came close to reaching an agreement-in-principle on land claims with the federal government, but the bands, sending a sharp rebuke to the Whitehorse-based executive, rejected it.

Special efforts have been made to ensure that the communities, acting through their chiefs, retain control of the CYI. Organizational structures are designed to guarantee that the central office does not lose touch with conditions in the villages. Under current arrangements, the chairman and vice-chairmen of the CYI are elected in Territory-wide elections. The chiefs, however, determine the positions held by the elected representatives. The annual general assemblies, although pre-occupied in recent years by discussion of land-claims issues, provide an additional forum for band members to question and challenge the Native bureaucracy and leadership.

Native organizations in the Northwest Territories have followed a similar path. Angered by a lack of consultation with federal officials, Native leaders assembled in Yellowknife in the summer of 1968 to discuss a possible federation of the sixteen Dene bands. The Indian Brotherhood of the Northwest Territories was formed the following year. Aboriginal solidarity held much promise for the Dene. As one Dogrib women declared, "They could ignore some of us, and beat some us, and steal from some of us, and pat some of us on the head before, but they will never be able to do that to us again, because we have our Indian Brotherhood now."

The Indian Brotherhood of the NWT, working with the Metis and Non-Status Association of the NWT (formed in 1973), pressed for a quick settlement of land claims. The proposed construction of the Mackenzie Valley pipeline fueled their resolve and gave strength to the radical wing of the organization. At a joint meeting of the General Assembly of the Indian Brotherhood and the Metis and Non-Status Indian Association of the Northwest Territories at Fort Simpson in July 1975, delegates enthusiastically endorsed the Dene Declaration. "We, the Dene of the Northwest Territories," the statement began, "insist on the right to be regarded by ourselves and the world as a nation." Such radical and dramatic statements shocked politicians and government officials, even those who were used to the passionate negotiations surrounding land claims. In their statement, the Dene asserted their nationhood and demanded a recognition of aboriginal sovereignty. In a breathtaking sweep through federal and territorial powers, the Dene outlined their determination to retain control over traditional lands and to ensure the survival of their language and culture.

The Dene also explicitly addressed the need for land claim negotiations. Although the area was covered by Treaties 8 and 11, the Dene argued that the accords did not resolve the question of land ownership: "The Dene regard Treaties 8 and 11 as covenants of peace and goodwill which served to establish a special relationship between themselves and the Government of Canada.... The Dene have never accepted the federal government's position that the treaties served to extinguish aboriginal rights to aboriginal title."

As negotiations to resolve the Dene and Metis claims continued, internal controversy pushed the Indian Brotherhood off course. The controversy revolved around James Wah-Shee, a Native worker with the Company of Young Canadians and president of the Indian Brotherhood from 1971 to 1975. Wah-Shee was a political moderate, often at odds with the more radical members in the association. To some of the left-wing, Wah-Shee had sold out to white interests by participating in the legislative assembly, which they viewed as an "alien institution." There was also considerable concern within the organization about the influence exerted by non-Native advisors. The conflict — personal, political and ideological — climaxed in the Brotherhood's statement in October 1975 that it had lost confidence in Wah-Shee. The president struck back, accusing Indian Brotherhood staff and outside consultants of interfering with the work of the organization. Having lost support, however, Wah-Shee had little option but to resign, which he did in December 1975. Tempestuous conditions continued until the next summer, when Georges Erasmus, promising to ensure community control over the affairs of the Indian Brotherhood, was elected president.

The 1975-1976 turmoil among the Dene reveals the tension in the newly founded Native associations. The role of consultants, typically white, well-paid and often southern-based, has been a matter of contention in all northern Native organizations. So, too, has the struggle between the Native bureaucracy, in this case personalized in James Wah-Shee, and the communities. Georges Erasmus clearly recognized the nature of the split, and saw that any successful NWT Native organization needed strong support from the chiefs and in the villages.

The Dene have moderated their demands over the past ten years, abandoning their quest for sovereign status in the face of federal refusal to negotiate this issue. The passion, however, remains very much intact. In 1978, at a Fort Franklin meeting, it was decided to adopt a new name for the association. Stella Mendo, a Fort Norman delegate, caught the sense of the meeting: "When we name our children we given them powerful names. Names that are strong. Our land is strong. Our people are strong and our people are one. We need a strong, powerful name to tell the world who we are. Let us call ourselves the DENE NATION."

The Dene have changed in other ways. They have abandoned their opposition to participating within the Northwest Territories legislative framework, particularly after the resignation of Commissioner Stuart Hodgson, the last of the old-style colonial administrators, in April 1979. The Dene Nation has maintained an active and prominent presence in the Territories, and not just on the land-claims issue. It has intervened on a variety of public issues, from oil-well development to proposed constitutional changes, seeking always to protect and enhance the position of the Dene people in the future of the Northwest Territories.

The Metis of the Northwest Territories similarly turned to political activism to defend their distinctive culture and to seek recognition of their outstanding aboriginal rights. The Metis have often had very different priorities than the Dene — their membership has tended to favour resource development more than do the Dene — and it is not surprising that the two groups have had their difficulties.

On its formation in 1973, the Metis and Non-Status Indian Association of the Northwest Territories joined forces with the Indian Brotherhood to present a united front to federal government negotiators. But the passage of the Dene Declaration in 1975 placed the Metis in an unfavourable position. The two groups could not agree on the status the Metis would enjoy under a Dene

Nation, a difference that eventually drove them apart. The Metis, moreover, were determined to protect their culture and identity, and wondered if that was possible through joint negotiations. The Metis withdrew from the Dene land-claim team in 1976, determined to negotiate on their own. The federal government responded to the Native impasse by cutting off funding, forcing the Dene to turn to the Anglican and Roman Catholic churches for emergency support. The Metis, who issued their own Metis Declaration in 1980, remained determined to gain recognition as a distinct society, although their political statements were far more moderate than the early Dene pronouncements.

The process described for the Yukon Indians, the Dene and the Metis of the NWT had, by the early 1970s, engulfed the entire North. The Inuit, widely scattered across the region, developed a number of their own organizations: Committee for Original Peoples Entitlement (COPE) for the Western Arctic, the Baffin Region Inuit Association, the Kitikmoet Inuit Association, the Keewatin Inuit Association, as well as the Makivik Corporation of Quebec and the Labrador Inuit Association. While these regionally based organizations provided a forum for addressing local concerns, there remained a need for a broader, united voice on matters affecting the Inuit. The Inuit Tapirisat of Canada (which means the Eskimo Brotherhood) was formed in 1971, with representation from six regional associations. ITC is a political and cultural lobby group, established to pressure governments to respond to Inuit concerns and to provide the Inuit with a strong voice in developments affecting their lives. Unlike the other major associations, however, ITC does not directly handle land-claims negotiations. In the Western Arctic, the Committee on Original Peoples Entitlement broke off from ITC in 1976 and negotiated on behalf of its people; the Tungavik Federation of Nunavut, established specifically for land-claims purposes in 1982, negotiates on behalf of the Inuit of the Eastern Arctic.

Organizations like the Inuit Tapirisat have an extremely difficult task in trying to draw the Inuit together as a national pressure group at a time when much effort is being directed towards local control and community-level leadership. With its head offices in Ottawa, ITC is well-placed to present Inuit causes to federal politicians and civil servants. The association is, however, having trouble interesting Inuit in its affairs. Turnout for ITC elections has been low, staff have become demoralized and complaints have been heard about the absence of powerful leadership throughout the 1980s. The current leadership, led by President John Amagoalik, is determined to emphasize the national role of ITC, leaving regional and local matters to other Inuit associations.

The role of Native organizations has been vastly underrated by non-Native Canadians. Interest has often focused on land-claims negotiations, a central function of most associations, leaving out the important work that CYI, the Dene Nation, Metis Association of the NWT, ITC and other groups have completed in other fields. They continue to devote much effort to political empowerment, urging Native people to assume greater responsibility for their own affairs. Native organizations have also played a major role in securing changes in territorial education systems, urging inclusion of Native-language instruction and cultural studies. Largely as a result of the political effort of the umbrella organizations, Native representatives have been included on a variety of social, economic and environmental boards in both the Yukon and Northwest Territories. Few of these gains came at the instigation of federal or territorial governments. That aboriginal people in the North have greater control of their lives now than they had fifteen years ago is due, in substantial measure, to the persistence of native political organizations.

Native Land Claims: The Background

From the early 1970s to the present, Native land claims have hung over the North like the sword of Damocles. For the Native people, the land-claims issue sits at the centre of their plans for social, political and economic development, and the reluctance of the federal government to settle the question of aboriginal title has been a stark reminder of the implicit hostility of non-Native Canadians to Native aspirations. Many non-Natives, however, particularly those in the resource industries, see the matter differently. To them, unresolved aboriginal claims are an unwarranted and unwanted interference in economic development.

The issue is not terribly complex. The Indians of the Yukon and the Inuit of the Northwest Territories have never been taken under treaty by the federal government. This was contrary to British colonial policy laid out in a Royal Proclamation of 1763 and Canadian government policy after 1870, which called for treaty negotiations before any lands were taken from aboriginal people. The government decided that potential developments in the North did not warrant the financial and legal commitments that accompanied treaty negotiations. The Indians and Inuit, officials agreed, were best left as harvesters, until such time as the pressures of settlement and development forced a change. Conditions differed somewhat in the Mackenzie River Valley. In Treaties 8 (1899-1900) and 11 (1921-22), both signed after resource discoveries suggested a possible development boom, the Dene were brought under treaty. From the beginning, however, the Dene argued that the treaty terms had not been properly explained or understood, and that the federal government had not honoured the limited promises made under the accords.

When the resource boom finally hit in the 1960s, forcing Dene, Inuit and Metis off their lands, and when intrusive government policies started to radically alter aboriginal life, the Native people responded. In the Paulette case of 1973, the Dene sought an injunction against future developments unless a land-claims deal was negotiated. Mr. Justice Morrow of the Supreme Court of the NWT conducted extensive community hearings throughout the Mackenzie Valley, listening carefully to the words of Native elders. He subsequently agreed that certain aboriginal rights still existed in the area, and issued a land freeze on 400,000 square miles of land within the boundaries of Treaty 8 and Treaty 11. Although Morrow's interpretation was overturned on appeal, the decision gave new life to northern land claims. And there were other signs that the Native case had legitimacy. The federal government's willingness to fund aboriginal land-claims research, the passage of the Alaska Native Claims Settlement Act (1971), the Nishga's partial victory in the Calder case (1973) and Justice Malouf's acceptance of Cree and Inuit title to Quebec lands in 1974 (overturned the following year), all indicated a growing acceptance of the need to settle the question of outstanding aboriginal title.

The Berger inquiry, of course, provided a substantial boost to Dene and Metis claims, specifically, and to aboriginal land claims throughout the North in general. As noted, Berger's final report called for the settlement of Mackenzie Valley land claims within ten years and for a suspension of major development projects until such an accord had been signed. The Lysyk Inquiry, struck to investigate the Alaska Highway Gas Pipeline, made a similar recommendation for the Yukon Territory in its submission to the government. The combined weight of reports by royal commissioners and generally favourable lower court decisions did not silence critics, who questioned why the government was devoting time and money to a process that slowed economic development. But it did encourage Native organizations to persist.

The path to a resolution of outstanding aboriginal claims has, however, proven tortuous and controversial, dominated by false starts, unfulfilled expectations, political machinations and internal struggles. The difficulties originate, in part, in the different parties to the negotiations: the Natives, the territorial governments and the federal officials. Their respective positions have changed considerably over the past fifteen years, resulting in an apparent rush in 1989 to settle many of the outstanding claims. That the process could take fifteen years is testimony to the rigidity of government positions, the vast gap between the initial Native demands and federal offers, the Natives' determination to strike a deal that provides the means for dealing with the future, and the unsettling influence of "third-party" interests.

The federal government carried conflicting motives to the early claims negotiations: a willingness to address its legal responsibility to sign a treaty with the northern Natives, and a desire to remove any impediments to future resource developments in the North. The government was insistent, from the beginning and to the present, that any land accord extinguish, once and for all time, any claimed aboriginal title to the land and resources. In its pamphlet of Native claims, *In All Fairness*, the federal government stated its position in unequivocal terms:

"The government requires that the negotiation process and settlement formula be thorough so that the claim cannot rise again in the future." Major resource developments, like the Mackenzie Valley Pipeline, were not to be held hostage by outstanding Native claims.

The government's stance on land claims has been somewhat clouded by its initiatives — or lack thereof — in other areas. The national debate over entrenching aboriginal rights in the patriated Canadian constitution raised serious questions about the federal government's commitment; Inuit children in Arctic Bay were kept out of school for two weeks in protest over the government's position. The promising Penner Report on Indian Self-Government raised hopes of a new enthusiasm for shared responsibilities, but the legislation arising out of the special commission died with the short-lived Turner administration in 1984. New messages also appeared from the Tory government. The Task Force to Review Comprehensive Claims Policy, chaired by Murray Coolican, offered similar support for aboriginal self-government, supported an elimination of the government's blanket insistence on extinguishment, and called for a broadening of the land claims mandate to include political matters. To critics who argued that the these proposals offered little to non-Natives, Coolican responded:

> Canada will be enriched if aboriginal peoples become contributors to Canadian life, rather than wards dependent upon the state. The economies of the region of the country will be stronger if their aboriginal communities are strong and healthy. Economic growth often has been dampened or new development delayed by the uncertainty of unresolved land claims. Agreements will resolve the uncertainty and will allow both aboriginal and non-aboriginal Canadians to benefit from new economic developments.

These were strong, encouraging words which offered hope to Native negotiators tired by years of unresolved discussions. Yet at the same time, the Natives' battle for constitutional guarantees of aboriginal rights and their enthusiasm for some of the ideas contained in the Penner and Coolican reports interfered with land claims. Northern Natives were, understandably, reluctant to make a final deal when it appeared that the federal government might relax or even abandon its negotiating position.

Despite Coolican's recommendation to the contrary, however, the government was not prepared to surrender its demand for extinguishment of aboriginal title. Furthermore, while Ottawa's politicians and negotiators were committed in principle to Native participation in planning and administration — the government was prepared to ensure Native access to wildlife and aboriginal representation on management boards and planning committees — they were often reluctant to surrender real authority to aboriginal organizations or bands. In this respect, the administrators were particularly guilty of foot-dragging. Not until the mid-1980s, and particularly during the tenure of David Crombie as minister of Indian Affairs and Northern Development, did the federal civil service truly accept the concept of shared responsibility. The significant steps taken over the last four years have done much to lessen the tensions within the land-claims negotiations and to indicate that a true realignment of administrative responsibilities is underway.

The governments of the Yukon and Northwest Territories have also played an important, although not always helpful, role in the negotiations. Initially, the federal government proceeded on its own, a situation territorial politicians found unacceptable. Many in the Northwest Territories were angered or frightened by the apparent radicalism of the Indian Brotherhood and the Dene Nation, and the territorial government, then dominated by non-Natives, opposed the Dene plans on land claims and other issues. At one point, in a deliberate attempt to challenge the legitimacy of the Dene and Metis representatives, the NWT government published a provocative pamphlet entitled *You've Heard From the Radical Few About Canada's North*. "Excuse us for being blunt," said one statement from the Territorial Council, "but we really feel that the Indian Brotherhood of NWT should be renamed the Radical Left." Similar scorn was reserved for the churches which rushed to the aid of the Indian Brotherhood when the federal government cut off its funding: "We appreciate that Canadian churches mean well by supporting the IBNWT. Frankly, though, we believe the churches have been conned." This position enjoyed considerable currency among non-Natives in the NWT through the first decade of land claims negotiations.

By the late 1970s, particularly with the appearance of a Native majority in Territorial Council, efforts were made to smooth relations between Native organizations and the government. A special committee on unity, established in 1979, sought a means of determining the wishes of Native people in the NWT and bringing those concerns into the political process. Understandably, much of this effort centred on the land-claims process. In 1980, the legislative assembly gave the Government of the NWT authority to participate in negotiations "in a way that is both cooperative and supportive of native rights, but is also responsible to all Northwest Territories residents including non-Native people." The government created the Aboriginal Rights and Constitutional Development Secretariat in 1980 to coordinate the NWT participation at the negotiating table.

The NWT position has, over time, become very supportive of the Native position. The government urged a broad definition of aboriginal rights and supported the Dene's longstanding position that a deal affirm, not extinguish, aboriginal rights. On the contentious issue of land selection, which the federal government wished to limit to traditional lands now used and occupied, the territorial government stood with the Dene, Metis and Inuit in calling for a more generous interpretation of the areas available. The territorial government also questioned some of the federal government's assumptions, as on the Natives' retention of sub-surface rights on lands they were not to develop: "It is nonsense to stipulate, as *In All Fairness* did, that subsurface rights be granted in order that they *not* be developed." As an overall objective, the NWT government declared, all parties should view the negotiations as a "social compact between Canada and the aboriginal people" and should seek an accord that was "open rather than limiting."

Conditions in the Yukon were, for much of the 1970s and early 1980s, less favourable. The Conservative territorial government, unabashedly pro-development, often expressed the frustrations of the non-Native people with the slow, tortuous progress of Yukon land claims. Yukon politicians had little desire to share power with aboriginal people, and protested any erosion of newly gained territorial responsibilities. Many were, to put it more simply, unsympathetic to Native aspirations and to the settlement of Native land claims. The hostility rested on several factors: misunderstanding of the Indians' position, unrealistic fears of losing land rights and the possibility that a land settlement would interfere with economic development. In 1979, in the midst of intense negotiations between the Council of Yukon Indians and the federal government, the Yukon administration introduced its own "land claim," demanding transfer of Yukon lands to the territorial government along with the settlement of the Indians' demands.

There were additional complications, caused by the extension into the Yukon of the COPE negotiations. The government under Chris Pearson was furious at being left out of negotiations involving territorial lands, and launched a publicity campaign in 1980 to outline its opposition to the COPE deal. Critics assailed the government's position, arguing that it misrepresented the issues and displayed a strong bias against aboriginal land claims.

In the early 1980s, the Conservative government of the Yukon continued to struggle with the land claims process, determined to protect the rights of non-Native Yukoners — the majority of the Territory's population. Concern was expressed, for example, that the Indians would claim much of the Territory's valuable mining lands; the government argued that a major portion of the revenue-producing land must be reserved for general use. The Conservative government had tapped a sympathetic vein in the Territory, for there was much support for their position. Its opponents argued, however, that the Yukon government was simply ignoring the inevitability of both a land claims settlement and a permanently enhanced level of Native participation in Yukon affairs.

The federal government, for its part, was not favourably disposed to the Yukon administration's demand for land. John Munro, minister of Indian Affairs and Northern Development, announced in the spring of 1982 that a major land transfer was not in the works. He was, however, prepared to consider a tripartite negotiation on constitutional development, involving both the Natives and the territorial government. After a bitter exchange, the Yukon negotiators walked away from the land-claims table, arguing that the "new pact between the CYI and DIAND clearly indicates a desire by those parties to negotiate additional benefits *after* a land-claims "settlement." This the Yukon government could not accept, stating that "to be fair, the land-claim settlement must be final" and that "aboriginal rights must be exchanged once and for all." Not all non-Natives supported the government's withdrawal from negotiations. As one commentator observed, "Many Yukoners were deeply disturbed by the Yukon government's political jockeying, which they believed showed both a lack of genuine commitment to Native land claims and a willingness to jeopardize the negotiating process and subagreements." But the government remained unrepentant. In the spring of 1983, it published a land claims information package, *Yukoners deserve a fair deal*. Chris Pearson summarized his government's position by saying, "We cannot go back to the table only to lend credibility to a process that is going in the wrong direction. We got involved in negotiations to ensure that a land-claims settlement will be fair to all Yukoners. We will not sign an agreement with which we do not agree."

The election of a New Democratic government in 1985, which found much of its support in the Native communities, altered the territorial position radically. The new administration backed the Council of Yukon Indians more enthusiastically and made greater provision for Native involvement in local and territorial affairs, a position the outgoing Conservative government had accepted only very reluctantly. CYI input was sought on a wide range of government programs, from a major review of the education system to the implementation of major federal-territorial economic development programs. While this level of involvement does not yet meet Native expectations, it is a major improvement over conditions of fifteen years ago, when Native people had little say in territorial affairs.

Conditions have changed markedly from the early 1970s. The maturation to a more moderate stance on the part of Native organizations, the increasing acceptance of aboriginal aspirations by non-Natives, the politicization of northern Natives and the accompanying softening of territorial resistance to settlements, and the increasing evidence of federal sincerity at the negotiating table have created an atmosphere conducive to the final settlement of land claims. There has already, in fact, been one completed settlement — the COPE agreement of 1984 — and several others are on the verge of being settled.

The COPE Settlement

The COPE settlement in the Territories involved the 2,500 Inuvialuit of the Western Arctic. The people of this region had originally negotiated through the Inuit Tapirisat of Canada, but in 1976, after a dispute over the structure and intent of the land-claim agreements, they separated to form the Committee for Original People's Entitlement (COPE). COPE applied to the federal government for separate funding to prepare its own claim, and in May 1977 it tabled a claim for 181,000 square kilometers of land, 133,000 square kilometers of water and a share of future resource revenues. The Inuvialuit also wanted power over education, game management, policing and economic development. An Agreement in Principle was signed in October 1981 at Sachs Harbour.

The pact, seemingly on course for an early acceptance, soon ran afoul of national politics. The election and rapid defeat of the Conservative government in 1979, followed by the re-election of the Liberals in 1980, derailed discussions. In December 1980, the Department of Indian Affairs and Northern Development indicated that the terms of the agreement were too generous, particularly with regard to sub-surface rights. Negotiations were suspended and only resumed in the fall of 1982. Then the Inuvialuit had to negotiate with the federal government while also settling overlapping claims with the Council of Yukon Indians, the Metis/Dene of the Mackenzie, and the Tungavik Federation of Nunavut. A final agreement was reached in December 1983.

Ratification votes were held in the Inuvialuit communities in May 1984; eighty-one percent of voters supported the accord. Parliament passed the Western Arctic (Inuvialuit) Claims Settlement Act in June 1984.

Under the agreement, aboriginal rights were extinguished. In return, the Inuvialuit were to receive $45 million (1977 funds), paid out in annual instalments between 1984 and 1997, plus almost $10 million to promote economic enhancement, $7.5 million for social development and title to 91,000 square miles of land. The latter figure included surface and sub-surface rights to 700 square miles around each community. Rights for sand and gravel, but not oil and gas, were granted for an additional 30,000 square miles. The Inuvialuit's hunting needs were also protected. They won exclusive right to hunt bears and musk-ox, and they were also to enjoy preferential rights to all other species except migratory birds. Representatives of the six Inuvialuit communities were also guaranteed participation on advisory boards responsible for land and resource management.

The COPE agreement set the parameters for future negotiations between the federal government and northern Native groups. The Inuvialuit settlement accepted the government's demand that the claim to aboriginal rights be extinguished; this issue has long been the major stumbling block in land-claim discussions. The final agreement also illustrated COPE's contention that control over land was more important than cash, contrary to what many non-Native observers expected. The rationale was simple — retaining ownership of the land is central to Native efforts to protect the traditional economy. The federal government was also pleased with the precedents established in this first comprehensive claim settlement. The COPE agreement acknowledged national control of the offshore, permitting unhindered exploration in the Beaufort Sea. The turning-point, however, was COPE's acceptance of extinguishment, a provision which guarantees that aboriginal rights will no longer interfere with economic development in the Western Arctic.

A land-claim settlement is a necessarily complex legal arrangement, involving financial compensation, definitions of specific rights and responsibilities and ongoing legal arrangements between the Natives and the federal government. The final accord called for the establishment of non-profit Inuvialuit Community Corporations in each of the communities affected by the claim. These organizations, in turn, control the Inuvialuit Regional Corporation, which holds all of the lands and monies flowing to the Inuvialuit. Several agencies were established to administer specific aspects of the agreement, including a Lands Administration Division, a Land Corporation, a Development Corporation, an Investment Corporation and the Inuvialuit Trust.

There were some protests over the terms of the accord. The Yukon government complained about the allocation of Yukon lands without compensation and a built-in preference for Inuvialuit contractors. A compensation grant from the federal government silenced the opposition. The Gwitch'in of Old Crow also expressed displeasure with the allocation of harvesting rights in the northern Yukon. Further negotiations between Old Crow, COPE, CYI and the federal government have resulted in an agreement on the establishment of a national park in the area north of the Porcupine River and a more specific delineation of Inuit and Gwitch'in harvesting rights in the area.

Problems also arose among the Inuvialuit. As Steve Kakfwi observed, "Although all the people walked into the negotiations together they didn't walk out together." There were struggles between COPE, which negotiated the claim, and the Inuvialuit Regional Corporation, established to administer the claim. Kakfwi commented, "In COPE it's really clear what happened over there. The main organization that negotiated the claim is disowned by the corporation that is set up to implement the claim." Although COPE retained its responsibilities for political and constitutional affairs, Kakfwi claimed that "the Inuvialuit Regional Corporation is taking control of everything.... [It's] moved them right out." In February 1987, an attempt was made to dissolve COPE and to transfer all of its assets to the Corporation. Roger Gruben, who initiated a successful resolution, argued that the Inuvialuit should be represented by a single voice, not by two different organizations.

It is too soon to gauge the full impact of the COPE settlement. The influx of settlement funds has coincided with the collapse of

Beaufort Sea oil and gas exploration, which, ironically,had spurred the government to negotiate a settlement. As a result, government and Inuvialuit plans to use the proceeds from the settlement to integrate local residents into the resource economy have not yet materialized. Still, the 1984 land-claim agreement provides the Inuvialuit with the financial and legal tools they long desired in order to control their own future. Only time will tell if these tools offer adequate protection for the residents of the Western Arctic.

The Council of Yukon Indians Claim

With the exception of the Tory interlude in 1979, the federal Liberals were in power throughout the early period of land-claims negotiations. John Munro, Minister of Indian Affairs and Northern Development, steered the COPE agreement through cabinet and presented an Agreement in Principle with the Council of Yukon Indians to his colleagues. The latter deal, however, did not move quickly to a final resolution, continuing a tangled and controversial process that had started in 1973.

The tabling of *Together Today for Our Children Tomorrow* was surrounded with controversy. The document included a critical review of Yukon history and sweeping demands for land transfers, financial compensation and guaranteed political rights for Natives. Many non-Natives believed, incorrectly, that the package represented the work of a small cadre of radical outsiders, and as a result were not prepared to support the negotiations. From the beginning, the pro-development Yukon Government acted as a brake on discussions, as it staunchly defended "third-party" interests in land and resource development.

Land claims were, however, really a matter for the Native people and the federal government. Territorial representatives were included on the negotiating team — and their influence increased over time — but Ottawa and the CYI were clearly the major players. In 1976, it appeared as though a deal had been reached. The press announced that a settlement, involving over $90 million in cash and large blocks of land, had been struck. The announcement, however, was premature and in the end actually

served to slow negotiations. Band chiefs, supported by the National Indian Brotherhood, believed that the CYI executive had
moved far too quickly, nearing a final settlement when many
people at the community level had only a rudimentary understanding of the issues at hand. At the May 1976 General Assembly, the Council of Yukon Indians voted to suspend negotiations.
The decision was more than a pause in discussions; it represented a strong signal to the negotiators and political leadership
that the communities had to be consulted regularly.

Pressure increased on government and Native negotiators,
particularly with the announcement of plans to build an Alaska
Highway natural gas pipeline. But the Indians would not be
rushed, and the federal government was reluctant to up the ante
significantly. In 1977, the CYI outlined its expectations — a
separate Indian government, authority over resource management and control over social and education programs. The
federal government rejected the sweeping requests, while the
territorial administration strongly opposed the Indians'
demands. As negotiations dragged on, highlighted by the
negotiation of over sixty sub-agreements but without a decision
on the major issues, Natives began to wonder if the non-Native
politicians truly intended to settle the outstanding claim. There
was increasing talk of taking the federal government to court, in
light of the fact that Canada had never signed a treaty with the
Indians of the Yukon.

The political will appeared in 1984, at the time of the COPE
agreement and as the federal Liberal mandate was due to expire.
Minister John Munro announced an agreement-in-principle early
in the year, setting the end of December 1984 as the final date for
the resolution of outstanding issues. The proposal, in exchange
for extinguishing claims to aboriginal title, called for financial
compensation and close to five percent of the Yukon's land.
There were to be additional guarantees of Native harvesting
rights and participation on management boards. The existing
negotiating structure required ratification by ten of the twelve
Yukon bands; by mid-summer, eight of the communities had
voted in favour of the accord.

But their excitement and sense of achievement soon dissipated. Even during negotiations, several bands claimed that the communities knew far too little about the details of the accord and their opposition to the extinguishment provisions threatened the deal from the beginning. The Carcross band followed through by voting against the deal. There was also increasing interest among the Yukon Indians for enhanced self-government provisions, which seemed possible in the wake of proposed changes to the Canadian constitution on aboriginal rights. By the fall, the CYI was demanding substantial changes in the land-claim deal, including a removal of the demand for extinguishment, more land, greater control over resources and the possibility of eventual self-government.

The election of a Progressive Conservative government in September 1984 quickly changed the structure and tone of negotiations. Although the new minister of Indian Affairs, David Crombie, made conciliatory gestures on his first post-election trip to the Yukon, it was clear that his cabinet colleagues were not prepared to re-open talks. Few discussions were held for the remainder of the year; Crombie even cut off funding for the CYI, forcing the association to lay off many of its employees just before Christmas. Negotiations did begin again in 1985, but in an atmosphere of confusion and distrust.

Anxious to prevent a repeat of the 1984 experience, the federal government restructured the claims process. Instead of requiring substantial support in the communities (ten of twelve bands), the government now called for the settlement of an agreement-in-principle with the Council of Yukon Indians. Once individual bands had selected their lands and negotiated specific terms in light of the Framework Arrangement, the land settlement would be in effect. Bands could, of course, opt to stay out of the deal but if they did they would not share in its benefits. The government also moved on other fronts, opting for band-by-band negotiations and declaring a willingness to consider greater self-government and resource-revenue sharing. The new policy was much more flexible than the approach taken by the Liberals, providing the community with "hands-on" participation in the negotiations. Natives were still concerned about such fundamental issues as extinguishment, but negotiations moved more steadily towards a resolution.

In the summer of 1988, the Council of Yukon Indians announced that an understanding had been reached on a tentative agreement, the terms of which were not made public. Several details remained to be worked out, at which time the pact would be presented to a special General Assembly. Pockets of opposition remained throughout the Territory. Some Natives were angry over the requirement that aboriginal rights be extinguished by the accord, and some were also dissatisfied with what they considered to be "secret" negotiations. In one particularly unusual — and unwise step — a petition was circulated demanding that the government submit any settlement to a Territory-wide plebiscite (where there would be a substantial non-Native majority) for ratification. Still, despite these signs of unhappiness, the resounding re-election of CYI president Mike Smith indicated general satisfaction with his negotiating style and the tentative framework agreement.

The CYI land claim is a particularly complex undertaking. Non-Natives, for example, have considerable investments in the Territory, particularly in the resource sector. Their interests have to be protected, but negotiators have had considerable difficulty defining legitimate limits on these third-party claims. In addition, the Yukon Indians are surrounded by other outstanding land claims: with the Kaska Dene to the southeast, with COPE in the north, with the Dene/Metis to the east and with Tahltan and Tlingit in the southwest. Overlapping claims are difficult to resolve, particularly when they involve on-going harvesting rights and land allocations.

The CYI and the federal government reached a framework agreement in November 1988. The proposed deal provides for over $230 million in financial compensation and will give the Natives control of over 16,000 square miles of land under two categories of ownership. Perhaps more significantly, the Framework Agreement provides guaranteed Native participaton in a variety of management and supervisory boards, ensuring continued Native input into the governing of the Yukon Territory. The focus now shifts to the band level, as community-by-community negotiations are required to finally settle the long-outstanding aboriginal claim.

The Dene/Metis Claim

For the Dene and Metis of the Mackenzie River Valley, whose struggles with the federal government have been even more contentious, the land claims process has followed a similar course. The Dene Declaration was perceived as being so radical and outlandish that the federal government cut off funding to the Dene negotiators. The expectation that a massive pipeline would be built down the Mackenzie River Valley, however, put pressure on the federal government to reach a settlement, particularly in the aftermath of the highly publicized Berger inquiry and amidst observations by some Natives that construction would not be permitted to proceed without a settlement.

By far the most politically radical of the northern land claims, the Dene/Metis negotiations were repeatedly interwoven with Dene demands for political autonomy. From the announcement of the Dene Declaration on aboriginal rights and demands in 1975, the Dene sought a political arrangement that, alongside a reasonable and just resolution of outstanding land claims, would assure Native people control over their future. For example, their plan for a new Territory called Denendeh provided for lengthy residency requirements for voting, guaranteed Native representation in the assembly, Native participation in resource management and aboriginal self-government. These proposals, intermingled with land-claims negotiations, slowed discussions and generated considerable concern and antipathy in the non-Native community.

Negotiations appeared to be headed for a settlement during the tenure of Warren Allmand as minister of Indian Affairs and Northern Development. Unlike his predecessor, Judd Buchanan, who dismissed the Dene Declaration as "gobbledygook," Allmand openly sympathized with the Dene and Metis position. He appeared, for example, to accept the Dene statement on self-government and seemed prepared to settle the land claim on that basis. In the fall of 1977, however, he was replaced by Hugh

Faulkner. Faulkner distanced himself from Allmand's proposal, offering a cash settlement and "reserve-like" land allotments. He balked at providing the Dene and Metis with control over resources. The Dene dismissed Faulkner's proposal as "totally ludicrous"; the Metis referred to it as a "beads and trinkets philosophy." Faulkner responding by cutting off further loans for negotiations. Discussions all but ceased until 1981. The negotiations were also stalled by heated struggles between the Metis and Dene leadership over the course of negotiations.

The 1983 election of Steve Kakfwi by the Dene Nation and Wally Firth by the Metis Association put negotiations back on track and the federal government restored funding for the negotiations. But the Dene/Metis claim, like the Yukon discussions, soon became tangled in a continuing maze of mixed messages coming out of Ottawa. The report of the Task Force on Land Claims Policy, headed by Murray Coolican, argued that Native people need not surrender aboriginal title through a land claim deal. However the Conservative government, represented by Bill McKnight, the minister of Indian Affairs and Northern Development, would have none of it. The government's demand for certainty — extinguishment — remained unaltered; this, to McKnight, was the *sine qua non* of the entire land-claims process, ensuring that the North would be truly open for future development.

With the framework for negotiations firmly and, it appeared, unalterably set, the Dene/Metis and the federal government continued discussions. Much remained to be resolved, including aboriginal interest in future oil and gas revenues, treaty rights, and land allotment. Finally, in September 1988, Prime Minister Brian Mulroney travelled to Rae, a small Dene settlement on the shores of Great Slave Lake, to sign a framework agreement with the Dene Nation and the Metis Association of the Northwest Territories. The deal left existing treaty rights, stemming from Treaties 8 and 11, intact, except where specifically amended by the new accord. It provided the Dene/Metis with $500 million (1990 dollars), as well as an additional $75 million mini-package relating to Norman Wells developments and a $20 million capital fund. Other entitlements included a share of resource royalties, special harvesting rights and guaranteed participation on management boards and title to 70,000 square miles of land (with 3,900 miles of subsurface rights).

The signing of an agreement-in-principle has not ended the process. Considerable negotiations remain before a final accord is reached, including band-by-band land selections and the resolution of several major issues, such as extinguishment of aboriginal title and aspects of Native self-government. Southern commentators were impressed by the size of the land transfer, repeatedly referring to the Dene/Metis as the largest private landholders in North America. But more impressive, by far, is the fact that the most radical and emotional of the northern Native land claims is nearing a successful conclusion. Surely this tentative accord is a symbol of how much has changed in the North — and in Ottawa — over the past fifteen years.

The Eastern Arctic Claim

If the Dene/Metis land claim is the most highly publicized in tne Canadian North, the negotiations involving the Inuit of the Eastern Arctic have received the least attention. This is not to suggest, however, that the Inuit, represented by the Tungavik Federation of Nunavut, have not made the settlement of this issue a top priority. James Arvaluk, president of Inuit Tapirisat of Canada, spelled out the Inuit perspective on their negotiations with Ottawa: "We are offering to share our land with the rest of the Canadian population in return for a recognition of rights and say in the way the land is used and developed." Much like other northern Native groups, the Inuit of the Nunavut have sought a lasting accord that accommodates their cultural and political aspirations.

Initially, the Inuit packaged their land-claims proposal together with a demand for political autonomy, through the establishment of the new territory of Nunavut. After a detailed study of their people's needs and expectations, the Inuit Tapirisat voted in November 1975 to begin negotiations with the federal government. It then tabled a formal proposal, asking for rights to large blocks of land and ocean, plus assurances that harvesting rights would be protected. The government was pleased with the proposal, which was a marked departure from the radical Dene submission. But the Inuit people themselves were not impressed, particularly with the suggestion that aboriginal rights would be extinguished and with the absence of a guarantee for political autonomy. Opposition from the communities forced the ITC to withdraw its initial proposal and to develop a new slate of demands, closer to the Dene position. But negotiations continued to go badly. The people of the Western Arctic, facing development pressure from Beaufort Sea oil and gas exploration, pulled out of joint negotiations and proceeded on their own (the COPE claim). Discussions with Ottawa reached an impasse, forcing the Inuit to re-think the purpose and mandate of their land-claims approach.

The Inuit, represented by the Tungavik Federation of Nunavut, approached the government again in 1980, and negotiations resumed. This time, however, discussions focused on a carefully considered Inuit proposal entitled *Parnagujuk* or "A Plan for Progress." *Parnagujuk* offered a sensitive compromise, avoiding rigid claims to oil and gas resources and demanding far less in the form of aboriginal self-government than the earlier proposal. Quinn Duffy commented: "The Inuit made it clear that they were in favour of economic and industrial development in the North and that they wanted to participate fully in the modern evolution of their Territory. They favoured future development so long as it was under Inuit political control and in harmony with Inuit needs." He went on to observe that "Rapid progress could have been made with this settlement and the process of negotiation of native claims revolutionized. But such progress required clear thinking on the part of the federal government, and that kind of clear thinking has been conspicuously absent in Ottawa."

While they were regarded by many observers as being the most pragmatic of the northern claimants, the Inuit did not find a particularly welcome response in Ottawa. Federal land claims policy, administered by a succession of different ministers and captured by the shifting tides of national politics, had trouble keeping up with the Native representations. The Inuit claim was further complicated by the simultaneous pursuit of territorial status for Nunavut, a process which promised to answer many of the Inuit requests for greater autonomy. Only with the clarification of government policy after 1984 and a government determination to settle northern land claims in the interest of opening the region for resource development, was real progress made towards a settlement.

Inuit claims to Nunavut have proceeded in a markedly different direction than other negotiations. In the COPE, CYI and Dene/Metis cases, government and Native leaders have emphasized the broad structures of a land-claim agreement, leaving the specific details and even some central aspects of a final settlement for resolution after an agreement-in-principle or framework agreement has been reached. In the case of the COPE arrangement, five years passed between the signing of an agreement-in-principle and the final settlement in 1984. The Dene/Metis and the government, who signed an accord in the late summer of 1988, anticipate that it will take two years of negotiations until a final agreement is in place. The Inuit, conversely, have already negotiated a series of sub-agreements, covering such issues as wildlife management and the protection of Inuit outpost camps (which must be included in the final settlement as Inuit lands). According to government sources, an agreement-in-principle on the Inuit claim is anticipated in 1989. Federal officials anticipate rapid progress after that date towards a final resolution of aboriginal claims in Nunavut.

When the Inuit of Nunavut first approached the Canadian government, they sought wide ranging political rights through their land-claims negotiations. Faced with resistance on that front, and recognizing an opening in another quarter, the Inuit proceeded with demands for greater autonomy through the division of the Northwest Territories. They estimated that the Inuit would form over eighty-five percent of the voting population in Nunavut, a guarantee that the Native majority would be able to govern in its own interests. The Dene/Metis responded to the Inuit demand with their request for the establishment of Denendeh, which would have provided province-like status for the Mackenzie district with specific guarantees for Native participation in government. Division, as already noted, seemed destined for success, winning the support of a majority of voters in the 1982 plebiscite. Conflict over the boundary continued, however, and the citizens of the more populated Mackenzie district remained lukewarm to the proposal. As a consequence, division remains on hold, awaiting a re-establishment of political will in the Northwest Territories and a resolution of several outstanding issues before the Inuit of Nunavut regain control of their political future.

Reviewing the Record

Native political organizations — embryonic, fractious and controversial in the early 1970s — have entered the political mainstream in the Canadian North. The Council of Yukon Indians, the Dene Nation, the Metis Association of the Northwest Territories and the Inuit Tapirisat of Canada are all major players in the governance of the Yukon and Northwest Territories. The land claims, settled in the case of COPE, at the agreement-in-principle stage with CYI and the Dene/Metis, and nearing completion with the Inuit of the Eastern Arctic, promise to shape the economic, social and political future of the Canadian North.

The last fifteen years have clearly witnessed a major re-ordering of political power in the Yukon and Northwest Territories. Native people have been fully integrated into the region's political structures. Natives dominate the NWT Legislative Assembly and, largely as a result of their perspective, have maintained that body's unique consensus orientation. Indians in the Yukon have not had the same political clout, being a minority in their own homeland, but they nonetheless exert a considerable influence on territorial affairs. Native people sit on most major boards and agencies, participate in community affairs and help to set the political agenda for the Territories. Such status and involvement represents a major advance from the early 1970s, when Native politicians and organizers were often dismissed as troublemakers and agitators. Clearly, non-Native Northerners underestimated the strength and persistence of northern Native people and the broad community-based support for the work of Native political leaders.

Many non-Natives believed, and some evidently hoped, that the Natives would not be up to the administrative and political challenges of the North. But they have been proven wrong. Through years of adversity and conflict, the Native organizations have changed and matured. They have moved rapidly from the radicalism and evident frustration of the early years to the confidence and determination of the mid-1980s, while still sustaining the passion that underlies much of their approach to government. There have been set-backs, such as the bitter Dene-Metis infighting, occasional problems with leadership and struggles between the communities and the Native organizations. But these difficulties stand alongside some impressive accomplishments, from the negotiation of land claims to the administration of Territory-wide Native programs.

Never again will Native people be pushed to the political and administrative periphery in the Yukon and Northwest Territories. Their voting power, aided by a favourable distribution of legislative seats, will ensure future Native representation in the legislative assemblies, particularly in the Northwest Territories. Agreements guaranteeing aboriginal participation on management boards and government agencies, negotiated separately or through the land claims process, assure Native people of a permanent voice in the administration of federal and territorial programs. Most important, the imminent resolution of outstanding land claims, to go along with the COPE settlement, provides Native people with the land base, harvesting rights and financial resources necessary to sustain traditional economies while participating fully — as partners — in the future development of the Canadian North.

Looking back over the past fifteen years, one can understand the Natives' frustrations — with confused federal governments, interfering territorial administrations and non-Natives anxious to involve themselves in land-claims negotiations. At the same time, much has changed, and a great deal of that for the better, as a result of Native activism. Of course, there remain many economic and social problems in the Native communities, as

Native leaders know only too well. Their work will not end with the resolution of the outstanding land claims and political debates. Rather, the battles of the 1970s and 1980s have been simply to win the tools and resources necessary to address the crises that threaten to overwhelm aboriginal peoples across the North. In the years to come, assuming the negotiations with the federal and territorial governments go well, Natives will be able to turn their attention inward and to address the pressing social, economic and cultural problems of the their communities. That they will have the resources and time to do so will stand as the true accomplishment of the past decade.

6

Northern Culture: Birth and Rebirth

Northern culture exists on at least two levels. On a national scale, there are the symbols of the Canadian North that find their way onto the bookshelves and coffee tables and into the art collections of thousands of Canadians. Inuit prints and carvings, Native handicrafts, published diaries of Arctic adventurers and books by Pierre Berton and Farley Mowat provide ample evidence of a national fascination with certain aspects of northern life. But culture also exists, obviously enough, for Northerners themselves, as an integral part of their lives, not as a consumptive good to be marketed outside the region. Here, in the vigour and distinctiveness of northern culture, one finds the strongest evidence of the vitality and potential of the people of the Canadian North.

Few northern artists or writers as yet command much of a national audience. There are exceptions. Ted Harrison's vibrant and simple paintings capture both the essence of the northern landscape and the imagination of southern consumers. A number of Inuit printmakers and carvers have solid international reputations. What is particularly distinctive about contemporary cultural activity, however, is the determination to harness that energy, talent and spirit for the North itself.

Education

External control of education is one of the best indicators of, and the most powerful means of perpetuating, a colonial relationship. If a region or social group is forced into an educational system that pays scant attention to its heritage or culture, the results can be devastating. In the years after World War II, Natives across the North were required to participate in an educational system that expressed little interest in, and certainly little sympathy for, Indian, Inuit or Metis cultures. The curriculum emanated from the south, supposedly offering Native children access to the Canadian mainstream. The problem, which was realized far too late, was that these same children would leave school poorly equipped for northern life and with little access to the world they had studied in the classroom.

The problems were particularly acute in residential schools. Children were separated from their parents for months at a time, placed in dormitory settings and expected to conform to a rigid and formal system of discipline and social control. The missionaries who founded the schools and ran them in the early years and the government administrators and teachers who followed them certainly meant well, but their inattention to the needs of their students left a deep scar that is still felt across the North. R. Lechat, an Oblate priest from Igloolik, described the problem:

> When a child has spent five, seven, ten, twelve years in school and thinks of getting out, he finds himself in a desert. Not in the promised and boosted land of plenty, but in a dry country, without water, I mean a *country without jobs*. For many, the end of schooling is even worse: it is an abyss of delinquency. The educated one knows no longer how to live in a country where there are no jobs, no work.

Conditions were, typically, much better for non-Native children. Most stayed with their parents and were educated in a school system which reflected their cultural traditions and personal expectations. But here too there was little evidence of a commitment to the North. Schools in the Yukon and Northwest Territories picked up the elementary and secondary curricula of British Columbia and Alberta respectively, and offered them with very few modifications. That was, of course, as the parents wanted it, for they had come from the south, expected to return there and saw their children's future in national, not regional, terms.

The problems of northern education ran deeper than curriculum. School principals and teachers were (and are) among the most transient of Northerners, particularly in the isolated, predominantly Native communities. For several decades, the pattern has been much the same. Teachers come north early in their career or perhaps for a break in routine. Few plan to stay in the North; only a small number set down roots and offer some measure of continuity in the school system. This pattern has been particularly evident in the smaller villages, which have little to offer university-educated, urban teachers. In such settings, turnover has traditionally been very high.

These are not new problems, and were in evidence before World War II. And there are abundant signs that the educational crisis, particularly for Native children, persists. But where, in the past, there was concern and despair, there is now action. In both Territories, Northerners are assuming control over the educational system, working to make it relevant and seeking to ensure that northern subjects are integrated into the curriculum. But these changes are very recent, and the problems of restructuring an established educational system have proved to be trying.

In the Northwest Territories, the Department of Indian Affairs and Northern Development operated the school system until 1968, when a NWT Department of Education was formed. This attempted regionalization did not solve all the problems. In 1981-1982, a Special Committee on Education held public hearings in thirty-four communities across the Territory. Over 1500 witnesses came forward to discuss their concerns about the educational system. The comments were, in the main, not favourable. Part of the problem lay with the unique expectations for northern residents: "Students should be taught the attitudes, skills and knowledge to be successful both in the traditional economy and the wage economy." There were particular difficulties, and much contentious debate, over language instruction. Some parents wanted their children educated in English, so that they could integrate more easily into the wage economy. Others valued traditional languages, and wanted them maintained as a language of instruction, not simply a classroom subject.

It became clear that the levels of instruction and accomplishment were not even across the North, causing difficulties for students and teachers in the regional high schools. Small community populations required older students to leave their homes for the larger centres, where they lived in residence while attending school. Concerns were also expressed about the high turnover rate of teachers — the average length of stay for non-Native teachers was three years and it was not uncommon for a region to lose one-third of its teachers and principals in a single year — and the lack of northern training for teachers educated in the south.

The committee offered a variety of recommendations. It called for expanded recruitment of Native teachers, cross-cultural training for non-Native teachers, improved adult education programs and far greater emphasis on the creation of a northern-based curriculum, including the revision of the school year to accommodate traditional activities. Echoing the repeated protests from the communities, it also called for the decentralization of school administration through the establishment of divisional boards of education.

The latter proposal generated considerable debate. There were, for example, no school boards outside of Yellowknife until 1985; local residents had to be content with education committees that forwarded recommendations to regional education councils. The residents of Baffin Island were unhappy with this structure. They broke away from the Baffin Regional Council and formed a Baffin Regional Education Society. In April 1985, the Baffin Divisional School Board was established. The distinction between a society and a school board is important. In the former case, the Baffin representatives simply forwarded recommendations to Yellowknife; as a school board, with a specified budget, they are now charged with administering their own affairs. Although Baffin remains the only region with a divisional school board, other jurisdictions appear to be moving in that direction. The Den Cho, Kitikmeot and Dogrib areas have been given funds to explore the possibility of establishing regional boards.

While the administrative struggles continue — difficulties with Yellowknife now replace earlier battles with Ottawa — there has been considerable progress made in the area of language instruction. Like other Native groups across the country, Native people in the Northwest Territories see the preservation of language skills as essential to cultural survival. At an Inuit Tapirisat Council meeting at Fort Chimo in 1977, for example, the Inuit requested instruction in Inuktitut, plus specialized training in traditional lifestyles. The Natives' requests were not ignored. By 1981, the Department of Education provided, when requested, Native-language instruction from Kindergarten to Grade Three. The language was taught as a subject thereafter. Still, development of Native-language instruction has been uneven across the Territory. Fort Franklin, an isolated Slavey community, has one of the better programs in the NWT; mixed settlements, with members of different Native language groups, have had some difficulty developing appropriate language programs.

The Natives have not left the preservation of language entirely to the educational system. The ITC established the Inuit Cultural Institute at Eskimo Point in 1973, selecting that community because of the high number of people still living off the land. The institute was responsible for translating English-printed materials into Inuktitut, compiling a dictionary of dialects, collecting elders' stories, creating new words for new technology and material goods and developing a school curriculum that would be of use to the Inuit. In 1981, COPE created the Inuvialuktun Language Project with a similar mandate to the Eskimo Point centre. A language centre was established in Tuktoyuktuk in 1986, funded through a federal aboriginal language enhancement program. Additional language centres were announced for Fort Franklin and Fort Simpson.

As the Inuit worked on the preservation of their language, they saw the need for a common writing system to facilitate communication between the communities. After considerable work, the Inuit Cultural Institute ratified a dual (Roman and syllabic) orthography in August 1976. The standardized orthography has been "a godsend to the educational system." Teacher training, the preparation of teacher aids and the development of audio-visual materials have improved considerably as a result. Word-processing systems have been created using the new orthography; computer programs have been adapted for class-room use. Further, the widespread acceptance of written Inuk-titut has made possible the publication of syllabic-based journals including *Inuktitut*, *Inuit Today* and *Nunatsiaq News*.

A similar effort is underway among the Dene. There are five Dene languages, but no standardized alphabetic systems as yet. The languages have Roman orthographies, produced in the 1950s and 1960s, and spellings differ widely. There have, as a result, been serious delays in the publication of Dene language materials. The Dene, like the Inuit, are working to address the problem. Committees made up of language specialists and elders are working to establish a standard set of Roman orthographic symbols and an official alphabet for each language. Further, a standard set of spellings is required for words. Such a project is extremely difficult and time-consuming, but its value is unquestionable as the Native people race against time to sustain their language and culture.

The Northwest Territories government has recently proposed an even more dramatic step. In 1988, the administration announced that Native-language instruction would be compulsory for all NWT students, Native and non-Native alike; successful completion of a program of language studies would be a prerequisite for graduation. This initiative, if passed (which seems politically unlikely), would raise the level of Native-language education in the Northwest Territories, and provide an excellent indication of the government's determination to ensure the survival and vitality of Inuit and Dene languages.

In some communities, the effort to make education relevant has expanded in other directions. Concerned about their young people's limited harvesting skills, the adults of Igloolik took action. They wanted Inuit teachers, and turned back two teachers sent to work in their community, replacing them with local Inuk. Caleb Apak, first president of the Igloolik Education Society, began taking the students to harvesting camps in 1980. After preparation at Igloolik, the 11- to 16-year-old children moved out on the land, where they were taught hunting, fishing and sealing and survival skills. The Igloolik action was not based on antipathy to other types of learning; rather, the Inuit initiative sought to give the children the skills necessary for their area, skills that would co-exist with the knowledge learned through the territorial school system.

A few parents have taken an even more radical step. Angered and fearful of the impact of sedentary life on their communities and people, some parents have moved their families to outpost camps. The movement, a small migration that began in the early 1970s and numbers about thirty camps in the Baffin district, was based on a desire to protect the children from town life while giving them the skills needed to live off the land. While the parents are reluctant to give up their camp life, they are also anxious to ensure that their children receive basic schooling. Several proposals have been offered to deal with this situation, including flying supplies and tutors into the camps and using the outpost camps as training centres for town children. The existence of such camps, although they are small in number, is a further indication of the Natives' determination to preserve their harvesting lifestyle and of their demand for an educational system that is relevant and responsive to their needs.

One of the more promising means of "northernizing" territorial education rests in the development of an indigenous teaching corps. The transiency of teachers continues to plague northern education; in addition, the southern teachers' lack of cultural understanding limits their effectiveness in the classroom. The best solution — for cultural, economic, social and educational reasons — would be to train Northerners as teachers. Native or non-Native Northerners would be sensitive to the abilities and problems of their students, would be more likely to stay in the area for an extended period and would be best able to adapt provincial curriculum materials to local situations.

In the early 1970s, the NWT established the Teacher Education Program, affiliated with the University of Alberta, in Fort Smith. A branch was later established at Iqaluit. The two-year program offered training in early childhood development, curriculum studies and in-class exercises. Offering little Native-language training and designed for high school graduates, the initiative at first followed a traditional southern model. But northern realities forced the course to be redesigned to suit the needs and abilities of northern students, and language instruction soon became an integral part of the program. The full impact has not yet been felt. In 1980-81, only forty-three of the 738 teachers in the NWT educational system had graduated from the program. Another 140 graduates were classroom assistants, mostly language instructors working with the Kindergarten to Grade 3 classes. While the northernization of the teaching corps is far from complete, major steps have been taken in a short time.

The development of education in the Yukon Territory has followed a different path. The dominance of the non-Native population ensured that educational programming deviated little from the British Columbian model upon which it has been based. Still, the standard northern problems — difficulties for Native students, transient teachers, and the lack of local materials for the classroom — hold in the Yukon. And it is here, in the schools dominated by Native students, where the greatest adaptations have been made.

As in the NWT, Native people in the Yukon have long voiced their complaints about a school system that, to them, seems irrelevant and unresponsive. Much of the impetus for change, therefore, has come from the Native community. *Barriers to Education*, a 1976 report by the Yukon Association of Non-Status Indians, presented the case that the territorial educational system failed to address Native aspirations and needs. The report called particular attention to the lack of Native language training and the almost total absence of Native culture in curriculum materials.

Some communities were prepared to take dramatic steps to get the government's attention. In 1978, the Kluane Tribal Brotherhood withdrew their children from the Yukon school system. They demanded direct funding from Ottawa, without the involvement of the Yukon Territorial government. At one point, the KTB temporarily occupied a part of the Kluane Game Sanctuary as a site for teaching traditional skills. The struggle ended with a compromise. The KTB provided a school building, staff and curriculum development and was to establish a school committee. The Yukon government retained responsibility for operating costs and promised to provide funding for further curriculum development.

As in the NWT, Native-language education has been the most successful and popular program. Under the direction of linguist John Ritter, and with enthusiastic participation from Native leaders and elders throughout the Territory, the Yukon Native Languages Project was established to study and promote the use of Native languages. The YNLP mandate was impressive: to train Native people to read, write and speak in their own languages, to develop a system for writing Native languages and to publish dictionaries, grammar books and reading materials in Yukon languages. The work of the YNLP has expanded into other areas, developing adult literary and conversation classes, collecting stories, recording place names and preserving local history. In 1983, Yukon College developed a Certificate course for Native-language instructors; in 1986, thirteen Yukon Natives graduated from the three-year course. Yukon Native-language classes are now available in most Yukon schools, although a recent controversy at one local school suggests that school administrators are not always supportive of the initiative.

Native concern over education culminated in the Joint Commission on Indian Education and Training, established in 1986. The commission cast a broad net in its investigation the problems and possibilities of territorial education. The final report, issued in 1987, found much to applaud, including the Native-language programs, cross-cultural co-ordinators and counsellors in the schools, the development of curriculum relevant to northern and Native students, and cultural awareness programs available for teachers. Still, the commission concluded that the existing school system fell far short of meeting Native needs. Most Native students still do not graduate from high school, and continue to feel uncomfortable within the mainstream system. Debate continues on the best means of addressing Native concerns. Some Natives wish to establish a separate Native school system; many object to a segregated system and argue that modifications of the existing school curriculum and structure could address Native concerns while preserving the integrity of the territorial school system.

The demand for northern educational reform extends beyond the elementary and secondary school level. Despite Canada's northern location, this country has invested comparatively little in higher education in the Arctic and sub-Arctic. There is a well-developed and innovative network of northern scholars, co-ordinated through the Association of Canadian Universities for Northern Studies (ACUNS). A number of northern research stations and government initiatives like the Northern Scientific Training Program have been designed to attract university students to the North on research trips. Yukon and NWT students wishing to pursue post-secondary studies receive generous grants (Native students are supported directly by IAND), an answer to a personal dilemma but not a solution to the absence of a post-secondary institution in the Territory. Until the 1970s, attempts to establish sizeable post-secondary educational institutions in the Yukon and Northwest Territories fell far short of expectations. That has changed of late, providing a vital boost to academic training and academic inquiry in the North.

The present Yukon College, recently moved into an impressive new campus overlooking Whitehorse, has gone through a series of transformations over the past two decades. Founded as the Yukon Vocational and Technical Training Centre, the institution offers a variety of career and technical programs. In 1983, the vocational school was transformed into Yukon College; a two-year university-transfer program attached to the University of British Columbia was added to the existing offerings. As the main campus expanded, Yukon College developed community learning centres throughout the territory. By 1986, Yukon College offered a range of academic, business, arts and technical programs. Building on its impressive and rapid growth, Yukon College was granted an independent charter in 1988, and is in the process of developing a Northern and Native Studies Diploma Program.

Post-secondary education in the Northwest Territories is more complex, reflecting the effort to address the basic educational needs of a small and scattered population. For many years, the NWT government's commitment to post-secondary education consisted, in the main, of grants to territorial residents. The sums were considerable; in 1986, subsidies for 354 students cost almost $950,000. Support in 1982-1983 consisted of free tuition, two return trips per year, books and supplies, forgivable loans (provided the student returned to work in the NWT) and supplementary living allowances for Dene, Inuit and Metis. Such programs, however, have helped only a small number of individuals — those with the academic credentials acceptable for southern institutions and those willing to relocate for up to four years while they pursue an education.

As in the Yukon, the development of post-secondary education in the Northwest Territories began with the establishment of a vocational school. The Adult Vocational Training Centre opened at Fort Smith in 1968, offering a variety of trades and apprenticeship programs. New facilities and programs were added over the years, many with a uniquely northern flavour. In addition to the standard academic upgrading, technical and business courses, the Fort Smith centre offered an Arctic airports program, training in renewable resource planning and preparation for work as a community service worker. The institution was designated as a college, Thebacha College, in 1981; the name was changed to Arctic College in 1985.

The newly designated Arctic College spreads far beyond the original Fort Smith campus. There are now three sites — Thebacha at Fort Smith, Iqaluit and Aurora at Inuvik. Thebacha, which specializes in vocational and technical programs, lost Teachers' Education to Aurora in 1987, although that program is now being adapted to a field-based study. The Inuvik facility, located at the old Department of National Defence, offers additional courses in business management and book-keeping. Tuk Tec, a joint venture by Thebacha College, Dome Petroleum and Employment and Immigration Canada offering training in oil-drilling technology, was absorbed into Aurora. The Iqaluit campus, specializing in adult upgrading, has only seventy students on site and another 200 extension students throughout Baffin and Keewatin. Arctic College, like Yukon College, is also making a major outreach effort; in 1985, the NWT college offered over eighty courses in thirty communities.

Twenty years ago, the Territories had little to offer northern residents anxious to pursue a post-secondary education. Those with the scholastic abilities, financial resources and personal motivation to continue their education received a sizeable measure of monetary support from the territorial governments, but there was little available for those who stayed in the North. With the establishment and expansion of Yukon College and Arctic College, and the continued development of distance, interactive and community-based courses, a wide range of business, technical and academic subjects are readily available throughout the North. The development is a vital one, sure to draw an increasing number of Native and non-Native students into the post-secondary network, a level of educational attainment once thought by many to be inaccessible.

The redirection of northern education, away from its colonial roots to a more indigenous system, holds great promise for the North. Educated in the history, language and culture of their own land, Native and non-Native Northerners alike stand to gain immeasurably. The opportunity to pursue a post-secondary education, at least in part, in the North also promises to attract many non-traditional students into the system. The new curriculum and priorities offer the North a solid foundation for the renaissance and expansion of its culture.

Preserving and Expressing Northern Culture

Northern culture is clearly at a cross-roads. For a long time the North, complacent in its status as a colonial appendage of Canada, was content to import its entertainment and culture. In recent years, however, Native people have demanded an end to this state of affairs and, in the midst of the political turmoil surrounding their land claims, have sought to preserve and enhance traditional culture. At the same time, although for very different reasons, non-Native artisans have begun to pursue their artistic ambitions in the North. The result has been the renaissance of Native culture and the creation of a distinctive non-Native northern culture.

The resurgence of Native culture, in a variety of forms and from many directions, has occurred at a pivotal moment. As alcoholism, suicide, illness and other crises attack Native society, the restatement of Native values and self-worth through expressive culture has provided a means of sustaining Native society. Part of this development rests on the perceived urgency of the situation. With Native language use in decline and the passing of elders connected to the pre-World War II era, there is great concern that the stories, legends and memories of earlier generations will be lost forever. The various language programs across the North, therefore, have the specific objective of gathering stories, place-names, and other oral testimony before time runs out. In the Yukon, for example, Julie Cruikshank of the Yukon Native Language Project worked with a number of Native women, helping them to record and preserve their stories and legends. This form of "rescue ethnography" has more than an archival component. The material being collected across the North fits nicely into new, locally based school curricula, provides documentation for those wishing to pursue further studies and engenders a certain pride among family and community members associated with the projects. A recent highlight of the new attention to story-telling came in June 1988, when storytellers from across the North, including representatives from Alaska, Greenland and Scandinavia, met in Whitehorse.

There has been a similar resurgence of interest in Native musical performance, often associated with fiddle and country and western music. In 1982, Inuit musicians from across the North met in Igloolik for an Inuit Music workshop. The CBC and, more recently, Native broadcasters, have encouraged this activity. Native musicians like William Tagoona, Charlie Panigoniak, Charlie

Adams, Alex Utatnag and others are developing sizeable follow-ings across the region. Summer musical festivals, the Den Cho Festival of the Arts held in Fort Providence in 1988, the annual True North Concert and the regular appearance of local artists on radio programs have led to a wider interest in Northern musicians.

Native artistic expression has expanded in other directions. There has been a particular resurgence of Native arts and hand-icraft production, led by the renowned Inuit printmakers and carvers of the Eastern Arctic. In 1976, arts and crafts ranked as the third most important productive activity in the Northwest Territories, a sign of its growing economic importance.

The Yukon has a similar group of Native carvers and artists, although they do not yet have the national following of their counterparts in the Northwest Territories. Keith Wolf Smarch, a young Tlingit carver, painter Jim Logan and carvers Fred and Allen Edzerza from the Dease Lake area of northern British Columbia, are but three members of an active group of Native artists who are rediscovering aboriginal skills and seeking to broaden their artistic horizons.

Although it is often seen primarily as a business venture, the production of Native handicrafts has an important cultural dimension. Moose-hair tufting, beadwork, the making of moc-casins and coats are increasingly targeted at the tourist trade. This work, however, affords Native craftspeople — the majority of them women — an opportunity to practise traditional skills, integrate Native and non-Native artistic concepts and interpret their world. The production of coats, to provide one example, illustrates the important cultural and regional variations in northern handicrafts. Communities and regions across the North — Inuvik, the Yukon, Pangnirtung, Iqaluit, Coppermine and Spence Bay — each have a distinctive style. Several groups — Iqaluit, Igloolik and Baker Lake — produce amautit (parkas with large hoods for carrying babies). The Spence Bay parka is par-ticularly renowned: "Its duffel is adorned with lovely natural-dyed wool embroidery, and buttons fashioned from caribou antler or muskox horn. The finished piece is so beautiful it's not even sold with a shell."

Northern art work, however, is facing a major challenge from the same animal rights groups and sentiments that have threatened to undermine the northern fur trade. When the United States tightened imports of whalebone and ivory in 1975, Canadian Arctic Producers complained strongly. The measure, designed to halt the importation of newly killed materials, cut into the Inuit artistic production. As the Inuit pointed out, the whalebone used for artwork was at least twenty-five years old, and the animals had not been killed for artistic purposes. Once again, however, the Inuit had been trapped in a legislative initiative beyond their control. Although whalebone and ivory carving continues, production has changed to include caribou and moose antler as well, items free from the exclusionary regulations.

The Native people have not been alone in their efforts to understand and interpret the northland through their art. Ted Harrison, a Carcross-based painter famous for the "studied naivete" of his brilliantly coloured works, is probably the best known. But Harrison is far from alone. Jim Robb, an unassuming artist with a practised eye for depicting the transition of northern life, has found a ready market in the North for his material. Others, like Sherman Hines, Richard Harrington and George Caleb, use photography to bring their vision of the region to life.

A few decades ago, the non-Native artistic impulse was almost entirely southern-based, left to travellers and adventurers who passed briefly through the North. Not surprisingly, their materials focused on the region's geography and not on human adaptation to the land. This is now changing. Non-Native art work has become increasingly connected with the North itself, generated in the North by people who call the Yukon or the Northwest Territories their home. Regionally based painters, photographers and other artists are now offering a more northerly-oriented interpretation of life in the region.

The development of cultural societies and the building of suitable facilities for the visual and performing arts have long been a preoccupation of cultural aficionados. The North's major coup in this field came with the opening in April 1979 of the Prince of Wales Heritage Centre, an $8 million museum and performing arts complex. Although NWT officials had long sup-

ported the idea of a major cultural complex for the territory, it was not until a band of southern supporters — cultural enthusiasts and philanthropists — threw their organizers and financial weight behind the project that construction actually began. The centre offers auditorium space, professional exhibits of the North's history and culture, consulting services to museums in smaller communities and a range of other professional and cultural services. There has been agitation in the Yukon for a decade or more to build a similar centre in Whitehorse; plans are now under consideration for the construction of a suitable facility on the campus of Yukon College.

Northern publishing is also struggling to find a commercial toehold. Costs of production and limited access to the crucial book-selling markets in southern Canada long conspired to limited the prospects for northern publishing. The barrier is now being broken. Heading the effort is a unique Yellowknife company, Outcrop Publishing, which has published an extensive list of northern books (the most well known are *Great Bear* and *Christmas in the Big Igloo*)and annual data books on the Yukon and Northwest Territories. Several years ago, they produced a magazine about the North, *Up Here*, marketed largely to southern audiences who are, in one observer's words, "attracted to an element of fantasy. Reading about the North is a surrogate experience for something they may never do." A second magazine venture, *Business North*, operated for only two years before suspending publication. The Inuit Tapirisat produces a monthly newsmagazine, *Inuit Today*, providing an Inuit perspective on the affairs of the region. The North is just reaching the point where it can truly start to celebrate its indigenous literature. That literature is still small in scale but it carries a unique perspective that until now has been missing in writing on the North. Kenn Harper's powerful story, *Give Me My Father's Body: The Story of Minik, the New York Eskimo*, is an excellent example of this, as is Jane Griffin's anecdotal history of northern mining, *Cashing In*, and E. Davignon's *The Cinnamon Mine*, reminiscences of her life along the Alaska Highway.

Interest in the North among southern publishers has not waned. Each years, dozens of picture books, memoirs and illustrated histories about the North find their way on the nation's bookshelves. Two of the most prolific northern Canadian publishers are, ironically, based in the United States. Alaska Northwest Publishing, based in Washington State and publisher of the famous *Milepost* travel guide, and Stan Cohen's Pictorial Histories Publishing Company of Montana produce specifically for the tourist market.

Only recently have northern companies begun to move in this same direction. The Champagne-Aishihik Indian Band and Sha-Tan Tours produced a travel guide to the Whitehorse-to-Haines Alaska roadway, *From Trail to Highway*. This kind of publishing initiative has the added benefit, beyond any financial rewards, of permitting the Native people to include their own culture and history in such guidebooks, a sharp departure from the other material available for the region.

The most vibrant publishing arm in the North, however, is that of northern newspapers. The region has a long and lively history of journalism. During the Klondike Gold Rush such papers as the *Dawson Daily News* and the *Klondike Nugget* entertained and often provoked northern readers. The *Whitehorse Star* has published continually since 1900 (its motto is "Illegitimus Non Carborundum"). The newspaper industry got off to a slower start in the Northwest Territories, due to the small and scattered population. A small sheet, *The Yellowknife Blade*, was run off in the 1930s and 1940s, proudly proclaiming itself to be "The Voice of the Voteless North" and "The Only Newspaper in One Million Square Miles."

Newspapers have proliferated over the past two decades. In addition to the papers in Whitehorse (*The Star* and *Yukon News*) and Yellowknife (*Yellowknifer*), there are a number of other regular publications. *Nunatsiaq News*, based in Iqaluit, publishes in English and Inuktitut and covers the Eastern Arctic. *News/North*, published by the owner of the *Yellowknifer*, offers coverage of the entire Northwest Territories. Native publication societies in both Territories have regular papers. *Dan Sha*, produced by Ye Sa To Communications Society in the Yukon, recently switched its monthly paper from a newspaper to a magazine format. *Native Press*, operated by the Native Communications Society, provides a similar monthly service for the Western Arctic, keeping Native readers abreast of news and community events in the region. And there are more: *The Inuvik Drum, The Hub* (Hay River), *Slave River Journal* (Fort Smith) and *L'Aquilon,* a Yellowknife-based French-language monthly.

While there is much to get excited about in the development of northern artistic expression, this output is often obscured by the stifling fog of North American popular culture. The widespread availability of television brings the culturally numbing images of mass-market America into even the most remote northern village. The onslaught of southern culture was, at first glance, both dynamic and exciting. Initially, television offered a great deal to people who had little practical experience with the world beyond their community or region. It offered a new variety of role models and vicarious experiences, a much different reality than the life of the northern settler or harvester. For non-Native residents, many of whom had been raised in the south and were familiar with both the medium and message, the introduction of television represented the maturation of the North, further evidence of the region's coming of age.

The effects of television on aboriginal people were quite different. What had been a relatively simple world, with few options and opportunities, suddenly became complex and diverse. For many Native children, the lives and situations of the television personalities offered a welcome contrast to the life of the northern settlement. Elders and parents were displeased, for the childrens' enthusiasm for the new images detracted even further from their interest in harvesting and northern lifestyles. That television dreams were, for Natives and non-Natives alike, almost inaccessible added to many Northerners' dissatisfaction with their surroundings. Introduced with much fanfare and welcomed enthusiastically in all but a few northern communities, the new technology actually represented yet another disruptive force.

While taped television was available in the major communities in the 1960s, live television did not come North until 1972, when the Anik satellite came on line. The Canadian Broadcasting Corporation added receiving dishes in communities across the

North; by 1981, almost every community with a population of over 500 people received the CBC Northern service. Igloolik, an eastern Arctic settlement of 700 people, was one exception; it refused the CBC permission to set up a receiving station until more Inuit programming was provided. The community relented in 1983 after the establishment of the Inuit Broadcasting Corporation.

From the beginning, Northerners, particularly the Native people, sought ways of turning the new technology to their own use. The Anik satellites formed the core of the new communications system, handling television and radio signals but also carrying telephone, teletype and computer messages. The Anik B satellite, with dual band capacity, was used in a series of experimental communications projects. In one instance, the Northwest Territories' assembly met in Baker Lake for an eight-day session. For two-and-one-half hours each day, officials were linked with their offices in Yellowknife, allowing the normal government operations to continue at great distance.

There were a variety of filmmaking initiatives in the early 1970s, designed to capitalize on northern interest in television. The National Film Board made films on Inuit artists like Kenojuak and Petseolak and enlisted the assistance of Northerners in preparing animated films on Inuit legends. Participants in a workshop at Cape Dorset, and a later one at Frobisher, worked with the NFB and CBC to produce northern Native films. Nunatsiakmiut, a non-profit society, began creating Inuktitut language programming in the mid-1970s, producing a number of twelve-minute programs and several larger special documentaries. Northern Natives, particularly the Inuit, were clearly anxious to capitalize on the new technology.

The Inukshuk Project, started in 1978 by the Inuit Broadcasting Corporation, established a television link between six Arctic communities: Iqaluit, Eskimo Point, Baker lake, Igloolik, Pond Inlet and Cambridge Bay. Production centres were established at Iqaluit and Baker Lake. The purpose was to permit people in isolated northern villages to meet via television to discuss common problems and concerns. Harvesting associations, health care committees, political organizations, politicians wishing to meet with constituents and other individuals and groups tapped into the service. The Inukshuk project also included a major Inuit training component. Trainees put together a variety of programs during the test period, including children's shows, a series on cooking food from the land and shows on folk tales, arts and crafts and public affairs. In the eight months of the Inukshuk Project, over fifty Inuit trained in various aspects of television production and more than 130 hours of Inuktitut language programming were developed.

The Inukshuk Project was but one example of Northerners' eagerness to capitalize on the opportunities presented by the new technology. Following on the success of this initial venture, the Inuit Broadcasting Corporation expanded its activities. Formed in 1981, IBC began broadcasting in January 1982. One year later, the company was producing five hours per week of educational, cultural and documentary programs. IBC had a major impact from the beginning. The founders recognized both the problems inherent in receiving television transmissions in the North, and the power to be had through television production. A technology that was doing much to undermine Inuit culture could, they realized, similarly be used to promote Native lifestyles, languages and traditions.

By the end of 1987, IBC was broadcasting seven-and-a-half hours per week of Inuktituk language programming, maintaining studios in Igloolik, Iqaluit, Baker Lake, Cambridge Bay and Rankin Inlet. Much of the programming, which is received throughout the Eastern Arctic, in northern Quebec and in Greenland, is largely oriented towards northern news and traditional pursuits, is broadcast exclusively in Inuktitut and makes a particular effort to develop suitable pre-school programming. IBC would like more broadcast time, and suffers from limited access to the Anik-B satellite, but that problem is about to be addressed.

There is also a Native Communications Society (NCS) for the Western NWT and an Inuvialuit Communications Society for the Western Arctic. These organizations are oriented primarily towards staff training and language development, so have not yet achieved the same level of production — or impact — as IBC.

The Yukon also has its own Native broadcasting company. Northern Native Broadcasting Yukon (NNBY), founded in 1981 as a non-profit communications company, has had a major impact in the Territory. NNBY began slowly, establishing CHON-FM, a radio station picked up throughout the Territory. In 1986, the company went to air with its first NEDAA ("Your Eye") program, a weekly half-hour news and information program. The following year, NNBY introduced special documentaries on such topics as teen suicide, residential schools and aboriginal land claims in the Yukon. The programs were well received in both the Native and non-Native communities, and represented the first effort by Yukon Native people to counter the barrage of southern, non-Native programming reaching the territory.

The Canadian Broadcasting Corporation has also developed northern production facilities of its own (the Native broadcasting companies have access agreements providing them with broadcasting time). The CBC maintains a production staff in Yellowknife and Whitehorse, preparing such programs as *Focus North*, a current affairs show, and *Northland*, a program on the cultural heritage and lifestyle of northern people. Approximately three hours per week of northern CBC programming originates in the region. Other northern programs, like *Targravut* (produced in Inuktituk), are developed in the south.

Northern communication services are not limited to regional television. The Whitehorse-based Cancom (Canadian Satellite Communications Inc.) operated fifteen northern receivers in 1982/83 and has expanded since that time. In 1983, the CRTC gave Cancom permission to expand its programming, giving it a total of eight channels (four Canadian, four American) and ten radio stations. Until the development of Native communications and Cancom, the radio arm of the Canadian Broadcasting Corporation had the North much to its own. The Northern Service of CBC radio began in 1958 as a small network of local stations. It now blankets the North, with radio production centres in Whitehorse, Yellowknife, Inuvik, Iqaluit and Rankin Inlet. Broadcasts are conducted in English and seven Native languages and reach throughout the North.

A number of northern communities maintain their own radio societies, a further adaptation of the new technology. The idea came out of Northern Quebec, where unlicensed radio stations transmit in Inuktituk. Most Inuit communities, operating on minimal budgets (often paid with the proceeds from bingo) and with simple equipment and usually volunteer labour, offer a modest FM service, playing music, making community announcements and keeping the village informed of the weather and hunting conditions. In the NWT, there are thirty community radio societies; in the Yukon, Carmacks, Dawson, Old Crow and Pelly Crossing have community radio services.

The central issue with radio communication is not access, but content. As with television, the proliferation of northern radio networks has helped to speed the assimilation of the region into North American popular culture. But these same networks, particularly the CBC Northern Service, have encouraged Native culture. In the early 1970s, long before the establishment of Native broadcasting societies, CBC offered Native-language programming from Churchill, Manitoba, Yellowknife and Frobisher Bay. Dun Quandro, in the Yukon, and Native Voice, in the Northwest Territories, were developed in consultation with Native organizations and offered Native affairs and language programs for their districts. The utility of having northern-based news media has been demonstrated repeatedly through the 1970s and 1980s. For example, the Mackenzie Valley Pipeline Inquiry, for example, was carefully followed on radio throughout its proceedings. (Most of the Native-language reporters working for the inquiry were later recruited by the CBC.) As Thomas Berger himself commented,

> In this way the people in communities throughout the North are given a report in their own languages regarding the evidence that has been given each day at the formal hearings.... The broadcasts mean that when we go into the communities the people who live there understand something of what has been said by the experts at the formal hearings, and by people in the communities we have already visited.

Later, the CBC Northern Service provided full coverage of NWT interventions on the constitution and in a variety of political, environmental and economic hearings. Perhaps most important was the extensive coverage offered to the complex debate over the division of the NWT. When the NWT Legislative Assembly held a debate on the issue in Iqaluit, the Northern Service carried the week-long debate live across the Territory. The CBC makes a major contribution to northern affairs. In 1986, CBC Yukon provided over forty-six hours per week of local programming, in addition to the national programming offered across the country.

Regional television and radio programming has clearly had an impact, breaking the dependence on the southern news media and carrying regular coverage of events and issues of primary importance to northern Canadians. Access to the international media has broadened the horizons of all Northerners, often altering images and expectations in the process. A study performed by Gary Coldevin in Frobisher Bay demonstrated that Inuit youth exposed to television were oriented towards the south in terms of career goals, travel plans, skills and preference for English. A follow-up study, after several years of Inuit broadcasting, suggests that there has been a return to a more northerly orientation. Native and northern responses to southern programming have had an important countervailing effect. As one commentator phrased it, indigenous television "allowed Inuit to break out of the bonds of the cultural imperialism imposed by southern television."

The commitment to expanded northern broadcasting received a major boost in the spring of 1988. The federal government announced that it would provide a grant of $10 million towards the establishment of TVNC (TV Northern Canada), a region-wide network that would combine the programming of CBC Northern Service with that of the six northern communications societies: IBC, Tagramiut Nipinget Inc., Inuvialuit Communications Society, Native Communications Society (western NWT), Ohalahatigect Society of Labrador and Northern Native Broadcasting Yukon. This network would free the northern communications societies from their dependence on access to CBC time, and provide for a region-wide television network. With the advent of TVNC, which is scheduled to go on the air in 1989, the North will have the best regional broadcasting system in the country, a strong tool to counterbalance the pervasive incursions of southern popular culture.

Forging an Identity

There is really not a great deal to distinguish northern cultural activity from the complex mix of government, professional, Native, non-Native and amateur cultural production to be found throughout Canada. And that, by itself, is a major point. Twenty years ago, the federal government was sponsoring tours by national performers — like Anne Murray and the Irish Rovers — to bring culture into the Canadian North. While interest in such concerts continues — symphony and rock concerts alike attract large crowds and music festivals have enthusiastic followings — the North no longer has to rely on imported culture.

Although far from complete, the transformation has been dramatic. Aboriginal skills and traditions, long kept under wraps by Native people who were only too aware of the hostility towards their culture among the non-native population, have been unleashed and are enjoying a renaissance. The more permanent non-Native population is also starting to develop artistic roots, seen in the paintings, writings and music that is proliferating across the North. Nothing, perhaps, is more important that the northern people's ability and willingness to capture new and advanced technologies for their own benefit. The development of radio and, more recently, television production in the North, and by Northerners, holds tremendous potential for a region that is struggling to come to grips with its identity and its future.

Epilogue

Fifteen years ago, Canadians paid scant attention to the Yukon and Northwest Territories. Oil changed that attitude and, for a brief time, the region seemed to hold the country's hopes for energy self-sufficiency. Then Thomas Berger and the Mackenzie Valley Pipeline Inquiry put a brake on hopes for rapid development. More important, the well-publicized community hearings alerted the nation to the aspirations and determination of the North's aboriginal peoples.

The North has changed a great deal in the years since the pipeline inquiry. Land claims, then wrapped in a cloak of Native anger and polemic, have been, or are about to be, settled. Native organizations, which initially felt the antipathy of the non-Native people and resource developers, have now been accepted as an integral part of the administrative structure. The federal government, once proud guardian of paternalistic domination, has loosened the apron strings, passing on substantial control and authority to Native people. Once outsiders in their homeland, aboriginal people now participate fully in the political life and government of the Yukon and Northwest Territories. It is easy, in the face of continued negotiations, arguments and struggles, to forget the impressive gains made by the Native people, and at their insistence. But those gains are very real and, in the short term at least, are irreversible.

The entire territorial North, Native and non-Native alike, has shared in the years of transition. In the early 1970s, both the Yukon and Northwest Territories battled against their colonial masters, demanding greater autonomy and less federal interference. The politicians and civil servants in Ottawa resisted change, holding on to the vestiges of colonial domination. But these battles, too, were slowly won by the Territories. Responsible government arrived, although in several different guises. In the Yukon, the introduction of party politics and the practical dethroning of the commissioner gave the electorate substantial control over its destiny. The Northwest Territories has, to date, avoided southern and foreign political models, preferring to preserve a consensus-style administration that seems particularly suited for the largely Native population of the region.

There are signs that this process will continue, perhaps not to provincial status in the near future, but to a point where territorial authorities can legitimately claim to govern their own affairs. On Sept. 6, 1988, Prime Minister Brian Mulroney and Dennis Patterson, Government Leader for the Northwest Territories, signed an Agreement in Principle on a Northern Accord. This pre-election deal, the final details of which remain to be negotiated, offered the Northwest Territories responsibility for the management of oil and gas and control over the revenues derived from these resources. While the accord stops short of "province-like" control of natural resources, particularly over the crucial question of administration of land, it provides the Northwest Territories with the ability to regulate and benefit from this crucial sector of the economy. In addition, the revenues from the development of these resources promise to free the NWT from continued dependence on federal government grants. A similar deal is currently under negotiation with the Yukon government.

Many of the benefits and changes, however, have been administrative and legislative, a vital underpinning for future improvement, but not a solution to immediate problems. Aboriginal communities remain in considerable crisis, despite unrelenting efforts to address the problems by local and region Native organizations. Frightening rates of teenage suicide, crime, alcoholism, wife and child abuse, medical problems and unemployment provide blunt evidence of a social and cultural malaise. There is, too, the particularly debilitating realization that most non-Native Canadians, in the North and outside, are prepared only to tolerate Native values, traditions and customs. There is little sense in the Native communities that their culture is valued by the public at large — a sad reality as they struggle to preserve their way of life in the face of unrelenting pressures to change. Land claims deals, self-government and devolution may provide long-term answers, but the current pain in the communities must not be ignored.

There are glimmers of hope: the restatement of aboriginal spirituality, the inclusion of Native cultural and language instruction in school curriculums, women's groups that refuse to tolerate the suffering in their communities, major advances in Native communications, the re-emergence of aboriginal medicine and the continued expansion of Native artistic expression. Against the background of these encouraging signs, there is a belief that the processes of cultural re-assertion and political affirmation will give Native people the skills needed to deal with a modern and changing world. But there is also a sad familiarity with the seriousness of the problems and only modest expectations of improved economic and social conditions.

The problems in the non-Native communities are less obvious, and far less painful. These are, after all, prosperous settlements filled with civil servants, resource workers and entrepreneurs. The non-Native population is generally well-educated and well-trained, and ready to take advantage of the many opportunities available in the North. Led by a core of bureaucrats, educators and politicians who are determined to end the boom-and-bust patterns and unenviable transiency that have formed the basis of northern life, the non-Natives have created an exciting and dynamic society characterized by its vibrant cultural and economic outlook. This group, far more than ever before, is also including the Native people in its plans for the future. While more can be done to integrate the Native and non-Native communities, major strides have been taken in the past decade.

It is, of course, the environment that defines the northern character of the Yukon and Northwest Territories. Despite the strong and seemingly inexorable forces of modernization, sub-Arctic and Arctic conditions will ensure a distinctive social and economic world. Development threatens the North's fragile ecosystems, particularly the offshore regions and transportation corridors, but the headstrong rush to exploit the region's resource has now been partially offset by increased environmental awareness. The merger of environmentalists' efforts and the Natives determination to protect the integrity of their land provides a potent counter-balance to the developers. There is still cause for concern, and an ever-present fear that renewed southern interest in northern oil and gas will overwhelm environmental considerations. The bitterly protested proposal to open the Alaska National Wildlife Refuge — site of the Porcupine River caribou herd calving grounds — for oil exploration suggests that Native groups and conservations cannot afford to relax their vigilance. On the environmental front, the North remains both a treasure trove of resources, to be developed in the "national interest," and a delicate ecological preserve, to be treasured and protected at all costs. The two uses are not, for the most part, compatible; the battle between these conflicting definitions of the North will undoubtedly remain at the forefront of political life in years to come.

In the mid-1970s, the Mackenzie Valley Pipeline Inquiry dragged Canadians vicariously into the Canadian North. The country learned of the persistence of aboriginal cultures and of the Natives' determination to survive as a distinct people. It discovered the inherent contradictions in the Native and non-Native visions of the North's future, as well as the diversity of a land often dismissed in simplistic terms. Underlying all of this, Canadians also were forced to face their role as colonizers, to accept the fact that their country ruled the Yukon and Northwest Territories much as Great Britain had ruled its colonies a century earlier. While there was no quick or easy consensus on how to address these political and cultural abnormalities, a surprising amount of effort and resources were devoted to finding solutions. Canada still has its colonies, and many problems remain. But much has been accomplished in the past decade and a half, perhaps more than Canadians might have expected, if not as much as Northerners need.

The North in the late 1980s is remarkably close to what Thomas Berger envisaged. Land claims are about to be settled, Native people have an assured role in future developments, efforts have been made to protect and enhance aboriginal harvesting and Northerners of all political and ethnic backgrounds are committed to ending the boom-and-bust cycles that have hampered social development and drained the region of its most valuable resources. The challenge of the next two decades is for the North to build on the promise and opportunity of the land claims and to fully incorporate the aboriginal people into the administration and building of the Yukon and Northwest Territories.

Canada's colonies remain just that, placated by generous government subsidies and partially seduced by the process of devolution. The assault of the Meech Lake constitutional amendments, which threaten to limit the region's evolution to political maturity and equality, is a bitter reminder of the North's constitutional position. So too is the continued refusal of provincial premiers to include government leaders from the Yukon and Northwest Territories in their regular First Ministers' Conferences. Northerners accept and celebrate their gains, recognizing that improvements have come in a comparatively short time. But they await more — they seek an indication that the Yukon and Northwest Territories have been completely accepted into the Canadian community, welcomed as partners, not tolerated as costly appendages.

Sources

This book is based on a wide reading of primary and secondary sources on the modern North. The Northern press was particularly useful. We relied heavily on such publications as *Yukon News*, *Whitehorse Star*, *Dan Sha*, *News North*, *Native Press* and *Nunitsiaq News*. The *Canadian Annual Review of Politics and Public Affairs* was also very helpful, as were the annual data books of the Territories published by Outcrop Publishing: *Yukon Data Book* and *Northwest Territories Data Book*. Much of the information on the Canadian North is contained in the hundreds of territorial and federal government reports published every year. Among the most useful are the statistical publications released by the Government of the Northwest Territories Bureau of Statistics and the Government of the Yukon Bureau of Statistics.

Individuals wishing to read further on the modern North face a wonderful array of choices. There are several journals which contain excellent material on the North. For the general reader, *The Beaver* and *Up Here* are likely to be of interest. Also very helpful are *Northern Perspectives*, published by the Canadian Arctic Resources Committee, and *Information North*, the newsletter of the Arctic Institute of North America. For those with more scholarly inclinations, such journals as *Arctic, Musk-ox, The Northern Review*, *Arctic Anthropology* and *Canadian Journal of Native Studies* contain much valuable information. Listed below are some of the more important recent works.

Berger, Thomas *Northern Frontier, Northern Homeland* Vancouver: 1988

Brody, Hugh *Living Arctic: Hunters of the Canadian North* Vancouver: 1987

Brody, Hugh *Maps and Dreams* Vancouver: 1986

Brody, Hugh *The People's Land: Eskimos and Whites in the Eastern Arctic* Harmondsworth: 1975

Coates, Kenneth and W.R. Morrison *Land of the Midnight Sun: A History of the Yukon* Edmonton: 1988

Cox, Bruce Alden *Native People/Native Lands* Ottawa: 1987

Dacks, Gurston *A Choice of Futures: Politics in the Canadian North* Toronto: 1981

Dacks, Gurston and Ken Coates, eds. *Northern Communities: The Prospects of Empowerment* Edmonton: 1988

Damas, ed. *Handbook of North American Indians Vol. 5: Arctic* Washington: 1984

Dosman, E.J. ed. *The Arctic in Question* Toronto: 1976

Dosman, Edgar *The National Interest: The Politics of Northern Development, 1968-1975* Toronto: 1975

Duffy, Quinn *The Road to Nunavut: The Progress of the Eastern Arctic Since the Second World War* Montreal: 1988

Hall, Sam *The Fourth World: The Heritage of the Arctic and its Destruction* New York: 1988

Helm, June, ed. *Handbook of North American Indians, Vol. 6: Subarctic* Washington: 1981

Honderich, John *Arctic Imperative: Is Canada Losing the North?* Toronto: 1987

Lopez, Barry *Arctic Dreams: Imagination and Desire in a Northern Landscape* New York: 1986

Lysyk, Kenneth *et al Alaska Highway Pipeline Inquiry* Ottawa: 1977

McMahon, Kevin *Arctic Twilight: Reflections on the Destiny of Canada's Northern Land and People* Toronto: 1988

Page, Robert *Northern Development: The Canadian Dilemma* Toronto, 1986

Paine, R., ed. *The White Arctic: Anthropological Essays on Tutelage and Ethnicity* Toronto: 1977

Rea, Kenneth *The Political Economy of Northern Development* Ottawa: 1976

Steltzer, Ulli *Inuit: The North in Transition* Vancouver: 1982

Watkins, Mel, ed. *Dene Nation: The Colony Within* Toronto: 1977

Wonders, William, ed. *Knowing the North: Reflections on Tradition, Technology and Science* Edmonton:1988

Young, David, ed. *Health Care Issues in the Canadian North* Edmonton: 1988

Zaslow, Morris, ed. *A century of Canada's Arctic Islands, 1880-1980* Ottawa: 1981

Zaslow, Morris *The Northward Expansion of Canada, 1914-1967* Toronto: 1988

Index

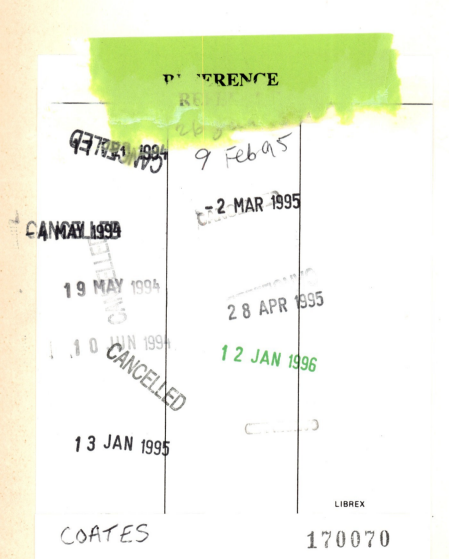